PET LIBRARY'S

German Shepherd

Guide

PET LIBRARY'S

German Shepherd Guide

by Madeleine Pickup

England

THE PET LIBRARY LTD

The Pet Library Ltd.,
Subsidiary of Sternco In-
dustries Inc., 600 South
Fourth Street, Harrison,
N.J. Exclusive Canadian
Distributor: Hartz Moun-
tain Pet Supplies Limited,
1125 Talbot Street, St.
Thomas, Ontario, Canada.
Exclusive United King-
dom Distributor: The Pet
Library (London) Ltd.,
30 Borough High Street,
London S.E. 1.

Printed in the Netherlands

ISBN 0-87826-413-2

Table of Contents

Cover picture: Sally Anne Thompson

Dedication

For all the Beloveds who have gone on ahead to where separation is unknown. Lord! There'll be deaf angels when we meet again and you leap up and bark!

A boy and his dog.

I   Why a German Shepherd

It is no accident that the German Shepherd Dog adjusts to most of man's activities — work or relaxation — since he has been selectively bred for some seventy years for just that purpose.

His harmonious balance, strong back and powerful chest, along with his lengthy, free and elastic movements were probably bequeathed to him by one of his sheepherding ancestors who spent long hours running after the flocks. His well placed shoulder allows him to turn quickly and easily when changing direction in pursuit of sheep.

The feet, too, are those of the working dog, well-knuckled with closely held digits, good thick pads and short claws. A longer "hare" foot is permissible but "cat" feet are considered stronger and more suited to his work.

Since the last decade of the 19th century when records were first kept, the German Shepherd has been gradually reduced in size from a large rangy animal measuring from 28 to 30 inches at the shoulder to a standard height of 26 inches maximum for males and 24 inches for females. With this reduction in height has come a heavier, more closely knit assembly of limbs, and a compact body well coupled; the angle of the shoulder and hindquarters, particularly the "bend" or sweep of stifle, is also more accentuated today although exaggeration is not permitted since any extreme of angles, fore or aft, would weaken the dog's action which is one of his outstanding characteristics.

In this change of physical appearance, the breed has remained recognizably the same, the chief difference being that it is smaller and heavier within the same outline.

The coat has been perfected too, and the highly prized "double coat" with the soft downy undercoat, and the shining smooth overcoat with the waterproof quality guard hairs lying closely over the back, are of great beauty and essential to the dog in his hardy outdoor existence; the body warmth is kept constant by the double textured coat.

There were some long-coated breeds introduced in the earliest days and occasionally their coats reappear to a lesser or greater degree, but while the standard does not state any length for the actual hairs, any long coat is invariably soft in texture with "partings" which spoil the weather proofing so essential for the German Shepherd Dog; they are, therefore, not considered typical.

The outlook or expression remains the same. It is perhaps one of the most difficult things to define and yet the most easily noted, even by beginners. The warm brown eye, sometimes dark, but always full of expression with a watchful, even questioning, almost human look: the well set ears giving an alert appearance while the proportions of skull and muzzle, together with the head carriage on the proud reach of the neck held slightly forward, give an air of great nobility and intelligence.

The appearance of the German Shepherd is always impressive by reason of his size and proportions, but the greatest charm of this noble animal lies in his character. He should be watchful yet gentle, courageous beyond description, obedient, and should possess undying devotion to his master, his family, or his animal charges. He is above all a dog to respect for his dignity and sagacity, a dog to understand and work along with rather than a dog to command in the expectation of blind obedience. He can be taught implicit compliance with his master's orders but his true greatness comes out in the manner he himself assesses his many tasks, and in his high sense of duty — truly a dog that can be all things to all people and one that will serve them gladly.

Their Keen Senses

German Shepherds so far surpass man in keenness of smell that it is difficult to imagine the nature of the smell sensations they receive. Just as it is probably impossible for a dog to imagine what colors are, so it is impossible for man to conceive of the vast range of odors and delicate differences in chemical shading to which a dog is so sensitive. In all animals, as well as in man, the olfactory sense is seated in certain nerve cells in a patch of mucous membrane. In man this membrane is confined to a small space in the upper regions of the nasal cavity. The dog has a much larger area of olfactory mucous membrane with many more sensitive nerve cells. Because of this, dogs can detect odors so faint that they are imperceptible to us. A dog that has been trained to do so can detect the difference between pure and salt water even though there is only one teaspoon of salt in thirteen gallons of liquid. A dog can tell the difference between artificial musk and the genuine product, although to the human nose the odors are indistinguishable.

It is a dog's ability to analyze odors which permits him to identify people on the basis of body odor. Any dog can do this to some degree, but the ability is greatly increased through training. A well-trained dog can retrieve from a pile of twenty or thirty sticks, the one stick which was handled by his master.

Dogs are far more interested in some smells than in others. Odors of animal origin have especially strong stimulative value, and dogs

American Champion Hessians Exaktor. Pictured here at 2½ years old, he has had an outstanding show career with many Best of Breed wins as well as a Group Win.

with no special training detect the smell of meat or urine in concentrations far below those to which man is sensitive. The guard dog depends partly upon his sense of smell to distinguish friends from strangers, and to distinguish his master's property from other objects. Never discourage your dog's efforts to investigate unfamiliar objects and persons with his nose, since this activity is one of the tools he must use to protect you.

Hearing

The German Shepherd's sense of hearing is superior to that of man in three respects. He can hear higher tones, he can hear fainter sounds, and he is (except in one respect) more accurate on localizing the point in space from which a sound has come. The one superiority of man's hearing is his ability to discriminate between different pitches more precisely and he can estimate more accurately the distance over which a sound has traveled.

The dog's keen sense of hearing is especially valuable to the guard dog. While his master sleeps soundly, he will detect the faint click of a burglar's tools against a lock, or will hear the distant footfalls of a trespasser.

A simple experiment can be used to show the sensitivity of a dog's hearing. If a small steel ball is dropped from a height of one inch and allowed to strike a metal plate it will produce a sharp click. A man with normal hearing can detect this sound when he is standing twenty feet away; a dog hears the same sound at a distance of eighty feet.

A dog's senses of smell and hearing do not completely "close down" when the dog goes to sleep. Dogs sleep lightly. Unlike his master, a dog will usually awake instantly and completely and be fully alert within seconds after an unusual sound reaches his ears.

Sight

It is widely thought that dogs have poor eyesight. While most dogs rely more fully on their senses of smell and hearing, the eye is not structurally inferior to that of the human. The canine eye is more sensitive to movement than to visual detail.

Color Vision

Experimental evidence supports the opinion that to dogs the world looks like a black-and-white photograph; they are, in other words, color blind.

A magnificent head study of a great American stud dog — Champion Hessians Baldur. A full length picture of Baldur appears on page 24.

American Champion Nicolette of Delray. Nicolette has a strong, powerful back, high withers, proper front and rear angulation. She is typically feminine and a powerful mover.

II   The Official Standards

In the pages that follow we give the interpretations of the German Shepherd Dog Standards that are official in the USA and in Britain respectively, as well as a translation into English of the German Standard. But first, we would like to discuss, in brief, the variations in these three Standards. There are no great differences but it is interesting to note which points are particularly emphasized and which are merely mentioned.

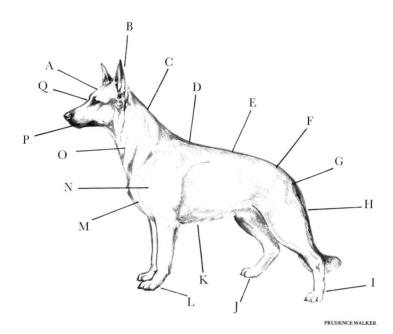

A. Slightly domed skull
B. Ears carried erect, moderately pointed
C. Neck, strong and muscular
D. Withers, sloping into back
E. Back, straight and strongly developed
F. Coin, broad and strong
G. Croup, long and sloping
H. Tail, set smoothly into croup and hanging in sabre-like curve to hock
I. Metatarsus, short, sharply defined and of great strength
J. Feet, compact with toes well arched. Good depth of pad

K. Abdomen, firmly held and only moderately tucked up in flank
L. Pastern, medium length, strong and sprincy
M. Chest, deep and capacious
N. Shoulders, sloping and flat
O. Clean neck, no throatiness
P. Muzzle, long.wedge-shaped with strong jaws
Q. Very moderate stop

The correct outline of the German Shepherd with the points to be considered.

The Three Standards

The original German Standard emphasizes the size of the dog, deeming an animal which is under or oversized to be lacking in suitability for both breeding and work. The British Standard agrees that the height (at shoulder) is 22-24 inches for bitches and 24-26 inches for dogs. It will help the beginner to know how far either side of this ideal height is acceptable as being within the Standard. So the British version is all right here, and we think the addition of the height range in centimeters in the German version a great advantage, since the breed is indeed universal. Neither the German nor the British Standard (although the paragraph says "Weight and Size") mention the correct average weight; but the Americans state that in proper flesh and condition a dog should weigh between 75-80 pounds and a bitch 60-70 pounds. Here I will express a personal view that practically all Shepherds in the ring today are several pounds above this weight, although height is fairly standard.

Character and soundness of mind and body, loom large in the German version, with the dog's natural courage and adaptability well stressed. The British call attention to the dog's impression of perpetual vigilance, his incorruptibility and ability to reason. The Americans urge us not to forget that the Shepherd's character is part of the combination of qualities which make up the true working dog.

The Germans speak of his alertness based on self confidence, his determination to defend himself and his handler or his handler's property if required, although he must be a well-adjusted member of the family — in particular, gentle with children and other animals, and at ease with all people. In addition, the Americans will not have him timid or shrinking behind his owner or handler, and neither nervous or uneasy at strange noises or sights, nor lackadaisical or showing disinterest in what happens around him.

A good dog can be constructed only on a sound skeleton.

PRUDENCE WALKER

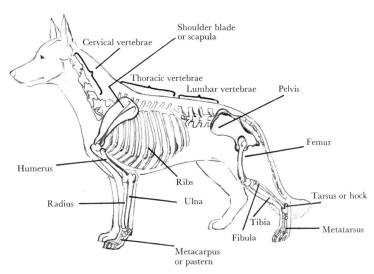

18

The British, also, claim that he should be alert to every sight or sound, with nothing escaping his attention. They say he should be fearless but with decided suspiciousness of strangers, as opposed to the immediate friendliness of some breeds. We prefer the American description of this particular characteristic; it says that he is not a dog to fawn on every new acquaintance, but at the same time should be approachable, quietly standing his own ground, showing confidence and a willingness to meet overtures without himself making them. It also mentions the "fear biter," snapping without justifiable reason because it is apprehensive of the approach of a stranger, a fault which is subject to *heavy* penalty. The Germans consider that apathy, weak nerves and any form of shyness render a dog unfit for the breeding program. The British do not mention weak character in their list of faults.

Both the Americans and the Germans state that eyes should be as dark in color as possible; but the Americans allow that lighter colored eyes are not a serious fault when they harmonize with the general coloring. The British concur, and add that the eye should be placed to look forward. This is intended, we imagine, to fault an eye which is placed up towards the corner of the skull; this gives a wolf-like appearance and is much to be deprecated.

Ear carriage is very important to the overall appearance and alert outlook of the Shepherd Dog. All three Standards are in agreement here, although the Americans think that the perfection of ear carriage should not be unduly stressed providing that the ears are fully erect. Some puppies take fully six months to attain their proper ear carriage, and the ears can go up and down many times during their major teething period — a phenomenon which often alarms novice owners. We find that when the ears are fairly large they take longer to go up, while a medium sized ear is usually erect when the dog is about four months old.

All agree that the neck should be well muscled and strong, but free from dewlap (loose folds). The Germans and Americans mention that it should only be raised up in excitement, "being normally held level," say the former; "forward rather than up," say the latter. This is an important point not mentioned in the British Standard, it being considered by many experts that a high head carriage on a long, graceful neck is the result of a steep upper arm, from which fault one also gets a prancing front action — another fault in itself. We have mentioned elsewhere that the Shepherd is a forward reaching dog —

HESSIAN KENNELS; GOSHEN, OHIO

Champion Hessians Tinsel is an outstanding show bitch. She was rated Excellent at the National Specialty held in Memphis, Tennessee in 1967.

the neck and head carried slightly higher than the shoulder, especially in movement, give him the correct outline and length of back (not to be confused with length of body, which is measured from the pro-sternum to the rump *through* the body.)

Throughout all three versions the greatest emphasis is placed on strength of muscle and firmness, as well as the well coupled body and correct angles, which give the dog his ability to turn quickly as is necessary in a herding breed.

Both the German and British Standards mention the necessity of removing the hind dewclaws if these are present — four or five days after birth is given as the ideal time. We do not like to see the front dewclaws removed as it gives a terrier appearance to the front legs.

The British deem color to be of secondary importance since it has no bearing on character or the dog's fitness for work, although they state that white or near white, unless possessing black points, is not desirable. We find the Americans in agreement here, expressing the view that strong, rich colors with definite pigmentation are to be preferred. The Germans, however, exclude from breeding *all* dogs with any white or true albino color.

Lack of sex character is strongly condemned by the Germans, and in the American version it is marked as a *serious* fault if the male is "bitchy" or if the bitch is "doggy." No mention is made by the British.

The Germans go to great lengths about the various types of coat, with three definitions, as you may read in their Standard. This is very helpful in giving the novice an idea of the range of coats which can appear in the breed, together with the reasons why only one type is held as correct in this essentially working breed.

Long hair in the German Shepherd appears to be a recessive characteristic, which crops out unexpectedly from time to time. Although there is no record of the Scottish Collie ever being used as a cross with the German Shepherd, it is interesting to note that today in Germany these long-haired specimens are referred to as "Scottish *Shäferhunde." Shäferhunde,* of course, is German for Shepherd dog, and apparently there is a belief that the long hair is due to a past infusion of Scottish Collie genes. Another extremely important point, which is given full mention in the American version is dentition, the number of teeth and the faults of undershot and overshot jaws being well described. Faulty dentition excludes an animal from the breeding program in Germany. The British make no reference to the teeth, beyond requiring the scissorlike bite under heading of *Mouth.*

A keen student of the breed can learn a lot of useful points by referring to all three versions and exercising his mind in the comparisons. There is plenty of food for thought and discussion therein. One conclusion will be obvious to all new students of these Standards, that a lot of things go into the making of a German Shepherd Dog — bone structure, proportions, correct amount of flesh, strong legs and feet, hard muscular condition and typical coat texture are a few of the most obvious points in this dog which is bred for work and intended for man's service. He looks splendid in the show ring, but even better at outdoor working trials. It is every breeder's duty to see that the German Shepherd continues in this tradition of strong nerves, good disposition and hard physical condition. "Prettiness" and "glamor" are for toy dogs. The proud looks of a true German Shepherd deserve more fitting epithets.

CLARE T. MATLIN; BROOKLYN, NEW YORK

This is an unretouched picture of American Champion Hexe's Bella of Highland Hills C.D. (Companion Dog). She is shown finishing her championship at the age of two years, under Judge John Neff at the Bald Eagle Kennel Club on July 30, 1967. The handler is Kim Knobluch. Bella is a recipient of the Dual Championship Trophy, offered by the German Shepherd Dog Club of America, for having finished both her championship and her Companion Dog degree within the same year. Bella was Winners Bitch — Best of Opposite Sex at the Westminster Kennel Club Show in Madison Square Garden in February, 1967.

And now for the three Standards:

THE AMERICAN STANDARD*

> **General Appearance:** *The first impression of a good German Shepherd dog is that of a strong, agile, well muscled animal, alert and full of life. It should both be and appear to be well balanced, with harmonious development of the forequarter and hindquarter. The dog should appear to the eye, and actually be, longer than tall: deep-bodied and presenting an outline of smooth curves rather than corners. It should look substantial*

and not spindly, giving the impression, both at rest and in motion, of muscular fitness and nimbleness without any look of clumsiness or soft living.

The ideal height for dogs is 25 inches, and for bitches 23 inches at the shoulder. This height is established by taking a perpendicular line from the top of the shoulder blade to the ground with the coat parted or so pushed down that this measurement will show only the actual height of the frame or structure of the dog. The working value of dogs above or below the indicated heights is proportionately lessened, although variations of an inch above or below the ideal height are acceptable, while greater variations must be considered as faults. Weights of dogs of desirable size in proper flesh and condition average between 75 and 85 pounds, and of bitches between 60 and 70 pounds.

The Shepherd should be stamped with a look of quality and nobility - difficult to define but unmistakable when present. The good Shepherd Dog never looks common.

The breed has a distinct personality marked by a direct and fearless, but not hostile, expression, self-confidence and a certain aloofness which does not lend itself to immediate and indiscriminate friendships.

Secondary sex characteristics should be strongly marked, and every animal should give a definite impression of masculinity or feminity, according to its sex. Dogs should be definitely masculine in appearance and deportment; bitches unmistakably feminine without weakness of structure or apparent softness of temperament.

Male dogs having one or both testicles undescended (monorchids or cryptorchids) are to be disqualified.

The condition of the dog should be that of an athlete in good condition, the muscles and the flesh firm and the coat lustrous.

The Shepherd is normally a dog with a double coat, the amount of undercoat varying with the season of the year and the proportion of time the dog spends out of doors. It should, however, always be present to a sufficient degree to keep out water, to insulate against temperature extremes, and as a protection against insects. The outercoat should be as dense as possible, hair straight, harsh and lying close to the body.

A slightly wavy outercoat, often of wiry texture, is equally

American Champion Hessians Baldur. Baldur is a powerful, flashy, masculine dog — a true working type — an impressive, beautifully balanced dog. Baldur was rated Select (Excellent) at the 1963 National Specialty. Also, he is a Register of Merit (R.O.M.) sire — sire of 13 champions, including the 1964 Canadian Grand Victor American and Canadian Champion Hessians Caribe.

permissible. The head, including the inner ear, foreface and legs and paws are covered with short hair, and the neck with longer and thicker hair. The rear of fore and hind legs has somewhat longer hair extending to the pastern and hock respectively. Faults in coat include complete lack of any undercoat, soft, silky or too long outercoat and curly or open coat.

Structure: *A German Shepherd is a trotting dog and his structure has been developed to best meet the requirements of his work in herding. That is to say a long, effortless trot which shall cover the maximum amount of ground with the minimum number of steps, consistent with the size of the animal. The proper body proportion, firmness of back and muscles and the proper angulation of the fore and hindquarters serve this end. They enable the dog to propel itself forward by a long step of the hindquarter and to compensate for this stride by a long step of the forequarter. The high withers, the firm back, the strong loin,* the properly formed croup, even the tail as balance and rudder, all contribute to this same end.

Proportion: The German Shepherd is properly longer than tall with the most desirable proportion as 10 is to 8,5. We have seen how the height is ascertained; the length is established by a dog standing naturally and four-square, measured in a horizontal line from the point of the prosternum, or breastbone, to the rear end of the pelvis, the ischium tuberosity, commonly called the sitting bone.

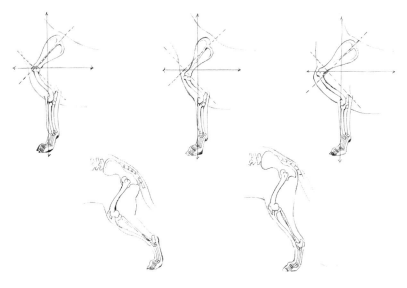

Angulation is important, both in the fore- and hindquarters. Upper row: left — Correctly laid shoulder; center — Steep shoulder (upper arm too short); right — Overbuilt forechest (upper arm too long).
Bottom row: left — Correct angulation of hindquarters; right — Too straight in stifle (croup incorrectly angled).

Angulation: (a) Forequarter: The shoulder blade should be long, laid on flat against the body with its rounded upper end in a vertical line above the elbow, and sloping well forward to the point where it joins the upper arm. The withers should be high with shoulder blades meeting closely at the top, and the upper

25

arm set on at an angle approaching as nearly as possible a right angle. Such an angulation permits the maximum forward extension of the foreleg without binding or effort. Shoulder faults include too steep or straight a position of either blade or upper arm, lack of sufficient angle between these two members, looseness through lack of firm ligamentation, and loaded shoulders with prominent pads of flesh or muscles on the outer side. Construction in which the whole shoulder assembly is pushed too far forward also restricts the stride and is faulty.

(b) Hindquarter: The angulation of the hindquarter also consists ideally of a series of sharp angles as far as the relation of the bones to each other is concerned, and the thigh bone should parallel the shoulder blade while the stifle bone parallels the upper arm. The whole assembly of the thigh, viewed from the side, should be broad, with both thigh and stifle well muscled and of proportionate length, forming as nearly as possible a right angle. The metacarpus (the unit between the hock joint and the foot commonly and erroneously called the hock) is strong, clean and short, the hock joint clean-cut and sharply defined.

Clean cut and strong, the head of the Shepherd is characterized by nobility. There should be a distinct difference between the male (left) and the female (right).

Head: *Clean-cut and strong, the head of the Shepherd is characterized by nobility. It should seem in proportion to the body and should not be clumsy, although a degree af coarseness of head, especially in dogs, is less of a fault than over-refinement.*

A round or domey skull is a fault. The muzzle is long and strong with the lips firmly fitted, and its top line is usually parallel with an imaginary elongation of the line of the forehead. Seen from the front, the forehead is only moderately arched and the skull slopes into the long wedge-shaped muzzle without abrupt stop. Jaws are strongly developed. Weak and too narrow underjaws, snipy muzzles and no stop are faults.

(a) **Ears:** *The ears should be moderately pointed, open toward the front, and are carried erect when at attention, the ideal carriage being one in which the center lines of the ears, viewed from the front, are parallel to each other and perpendicular to the ground. Puppies usually do not permanently raise their ears until the fourth or sixth month, and sometimes not until later. Cropped and hanging ears are to be discarded. The well-placed and well-carried ear of a size in proportion to the skull materially adds to the general appearance of the Shepherd. Neither too large nor too small ears are desirable. Too much stress, however, should not be laid on perfection of carriage if the ears are fully erect.*

American Champion Rolf of Delray. A very masculine dog, Rolf has excellent front and rear angulation. He is a powerful mover and excellent type.

(b) Eyes: *Of medium size, almond shaped, set a little obliquely and not protruding. The color is dark as possible. Eyes of lighter color are sometimes found and are not a serious fault if they harmonize with the general coloration, but a dark brown eye is always to be prefered. The expression should be keen, intelligent and composed.*

(c) Teeth: *The strong teeth, 42 in number, 20 upper and 22 lower, are strongly developed and meet in a scissor grip in which part of the inner surface of the upper teeth meets and engages part of the outer surface of the lower teeth. This type of bite gives a more powerful grip than one in which the edges of the teeth meet directly, and is subject to less wear. The dog is overshot when the lower teeth fail to engage the inner surfaces of the upper teeth. This is a serious fault. The reverse condition - an undershot - jaw is a very serious fault. While missing premolars are frequently observed, complete dentition is decidedly to be preferred. So-called distemper teeth and discolored teeth are faults whose seriousness varies with the degree of departure from the desired sound, white coloring. Teeth broken by accident should not be severely penalized but worn teeth, especially the incisors are often indicative of the lack of a proper scissor bite, although some allowance should be made for age.*

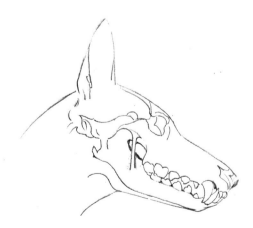

PRUDENCE WALKER

The correct scissors bite.

Neck: *The neck is strong and muscular, clean-cut and relatively long, proportionate to the size of the head and without loose folds of skin. When the dog is at attention or excited the head is raised and the neck carried high, otherwise typical carriage of the head is forward rather than up and but little higher than the top of the shoulder, particularly in motion.*

Top Line: (a) Withers: *The Withers should be higher than and sloping into the level back to enable a proper attachment of the shoulder blades.*

(b) Back: *The back should be straight and very strongly developed without sag or roach, the section from the wither to the croup being relatively short. (The desirable long proportion of the Shepherd Dog is not derived from a long back but from overall length with relation to height, which is achieved by breadth of forequarter and hindquarter view from the side.)*

(c) Loin: *Viewed from the top, broad and strong, blending smoothly into the back without undue length between the last rib and the thigh, when viewed from the side.*

(d) Croup: *Should be long and gradually sloping. Too level or flat a croup prevents proper functioning of the hindquarter which must be able to reach well under the body. A steep croup also limits the action of the hindquarter.*

PRUDENCE WALKER

Tail carriage is important but can vary according to the mood of the dog. On the left, we see the tail carriage permitted when the dog is at rest; center, with the dog in action; right, when the dog is excited.

(e) Tail: *Bushy, with the last vertebra extended at least to the hock joint, and usually below. Set smoothly into the croup and low rather than high. At rest the tail hangs in a slight curve like a sabre. A slight hook — sometimes carried to one side — is faulty only to the extent that it mars general appearance. When the dog* *is excited or in motion, the curve is accentuated and the tail raised, but it should never be lifted beyond a line at right angles with the line of the back. Docked tails, or those which have been operated upon to prevent curling, disqualify. Tails too short, or with clumpy ends due to the ankylosis or growing together of the vertebrae, are serious faults.*

HESSIAN KENNELS; GOSHEN, OHIO

In 1963 Champion Hessians Vogue R.O.M. was chosen the top bitch in the United States.

Body: *The whole structure of the body gives an impression of depth and solidity without bulkiness.*

(a) **Forechest**: *Commencing at the prosternum, should be well filled and carried well down between the legs with no sense of hollowness.*

(b) **Chest**: *Deep and capacious with ample room for lungs and heart. Well carried forward, with the prosternum, or process of the breast bone, showing ahead of the shoulder when the dog is viewed from the side.*

(c) **Ribs**: *Should be well-sprung and long, neither barrel shaped nor too flat, and carried down to the breast bone which reaches to the elbow. Correct ribbing allows the elbow to move back freely when the dog is at a trot, while too round a rib causes interference and throws the elbow out. Ribbing should be carried well back so that loin and flank are relatively short.*

The first impression of a good German Shepherd Dog is that of a strong, agile, well-muscled animal, alert and full of life. He should both be, and appear to be, well balanced, with harmonious development of the forequarters and hindquarters.

(d) Abdomen: *Firmly held and not paunchy. The bottom line of the Shepherd is only moderately tucked up in flank, never like that of a Greyhound*

Legs: *(a) The bone of the legs should be straight, oval rather than round or flat and free from sponginess. Its development should be in proportion to the size of the dog and contribute to the overall impression of substance without grossness. Crooked leg bones and any malformation such as, for example, that caused by rickets, should be penalized.*

(b) Pastern: Should be of medium length, strong and springy. Much more spring of pastern is desirable in the Shepherd Dog than in many other breeds as it contributes to the ease and elasticity of the trotting gait. The upright terrier pastern is definitely undesirable.

(c) Metacarpus (The so-called "hock"): Short, clean, sharply defined and of great strenght. This is the fulcrum upon which much of the forward movement of the dog depends. Cow hocks

31

The British Standard for the German Shepherd tells us that "The characteristic expression of the German Shepherd gives the impression of perpetual vigilance, fidelity, liveliness and watchfulness, alert to every sight and sound, with nothing escaping attention."

The hindquarters should be short, clean, sharply defined and of great strength (left). Weak hindquarters, as shown on the right (cow hocks), are undesirable.

are a decided fault but before penalizing for cow hocks, it should be definitely determined, with the animal in motion, that the dog has this fault, since many good dogs with exceptionally good hindquarter angulation occasionally stand so as to give the impression of cow hockedness which is not actually present.

(d) *Feet:* Rather short, compact, with toes well arched, pads thick and hard, nails short and strong. The ideal foot is extremely strong with good gripping power and plenty of depth of pad. The so-called cat-foot, or terrier foot, is not desirable. The thin, spread or hare-foot is, however, still more undesirable.

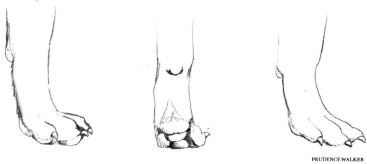

PRUDENCE WALKER

The feet are very important to the working dog. Left and center, we see well-cushioned toes which give our Shepherd his typically springy step. At right is a thin, flat foot which is undesirable.

Pigment: The German Shepherd Dog differs widely in color and all colors are permissible. Generally speaking, strong rich colors are to be preferred, with definite pigmentation and without the appearance of a washed-out color. White dogs are not desirable, and are to be disqualified if showing albino characteristics.

Gait: (a) *General Impression:* The gait of the German Shepherd Dog is outreaching, elastic, seemingly without effort, smooth and rhythmic. At a walk it covers a great deal of ground, with long step of both hind and foreleg. At a trot, the dog covers still more ground and moves powerfully but easily with a beautiful coordination of back and limbs so that, in the best examples, the gait appears to be the steady motion of a well-lubricated machine. The feet travel close to the ground, and neither fore nor hind feet should lift high on either forward reach or backward push.

Champion Marlo of Delray has excellent type, strong back, proper front and rear angulation, good head and expression — very masculine.

(b) The hindquarter delivers, through the back, a powerful forward thrust which slightly lifts the whole animal and drives the body forward. Reaching far under, and passing the imprint left by the front foot, the string arched hind foot takes hold of the ground; then hock, stifle and upper thigh come into play and sweep back, the stroke of the hind leg finishing with the foot still close to the ground in a smooth follow-through. The over-reach of the hindquarter usually necessitates one hind foot passing outside and the other hind foot passing inside the track of the forefeet and such action is not faulty unless locomotion is crabwise with the dog's body sideways out of the normal straight line.

(c) In order to achieve ideal movement of this kind, there must be full muscular coordination throughout the structure with the action of the muscles and ligaments positive, regular and accurate.

(d) Back transmission: The typical smooth, flowing gait of the Shepherd Dog cannot be maintained without great strength and firmness (which does not mean stiffness) of back. The whole

effort of the hindquarter is transmitted to the forequarter through the muscular and bony structure of the loin, back and withers. At full trot, the back must remain firm and level without sway, roll, whip or roach.

(e) To compensate for the forward motion imparted by the hindquarter, the shoulder should open to its full extent - the desirability of good shoulder angulation now becomes apparent - and the forelegs should reach out in a stride balancing that of the hindquarter. A steep shoulder will cause the dog either to stumble or to raise the forelegs very high in an effort to coordinate with the hindquarter, which is impossible when shoulder structure is faulty. A serious gait fault results when a dog moves too low in front, presenting an unlevel topline with the wither lower than the hips.

(f) The Shepherd Dog does not track on widely separated parallel lines as does the terrier but brings the feet inward toward the middle line of the body when at the trot in order to maintain balance. For this reason a dog, viewed from the front or rear when in motion will often seem to travel close. This is not a fault if the feet do not strike or cross, or if the knees or shoulders are not thrown out, but the feet and hocks should be parallel even if close together.

(g) The excellence of gait must also be evaluated by viewing from the side the effortless, properly coordinated covering of ground.

Character: As has been noted before, the Shepherd Dog is not one that fawns upon every new acquaintance. At the same time, it should be approachable, quietly standing its ground and showing confidence and a willingness to meet overtures without itself making them. It should be poised, but when the occasion demands, eager and alert: both fit and willing to serve in any capacity as companion, watch dog, blind leader, herding dog or guardian whichever the circumstances may demand.

The Shepherd Dog must not be timid, shrinking be-hind its master or handler: nervous, looking about or upward with anxious expression or showing nervous reactions to strange counds or sights, nor lackadaisical, sluggish or manifestly disinterested in what goes on about him. Lack of confidence under any surroundings is not typical of good character: cases of extreme trimidity and nervous unbalance sometimes give a dog

Clean cut and strong, the head of the Shepherd characterizes nobility.

an apparent but totally unreal courage, and it becomes a "fear biter," snapping not for any justifiable reason but because it is apprehensive of the approach of a stranger. This is a serious fault subject to heavy penalty.

In summary: It should never be forgotten that the ideal Shepherd is a working animal, which must have an incorruptible character combined with body and gait suitable for the arduous work which constitutes its primary purpose. All its qualities should be weighed in respect to their contribution to such work, and while no compromise should be permitted with regard to its working potentiality, the dog must nevertheless possess a high degree of beauty and nobility.

Faults: (*Note — Faults are important in the order of their group, as per group headings, irrespective of their position in each group*).

Disqualifying faults: *Albino characteristics. Cropped ears. Hanging ears (as in a hound). Docked tails. Monorchidism. Cryptorchidism.*

Very Serious Faults: *Major Faults of Temperament. Undershot lower jaw.*

Serious Faults: *Faults of Balance and Proportion. Poor gait, viewed either from front, rear or side. Marked deficiency of substance (Bone or Body). Bitchy male dogs. Faulty backs. Too level or too short croup. Long and weak loin. Very bad feet. Ring Tails. Tails much too short. Rickety condition. More than four missing premolars or any other missing teeth, unless due to accident. Lack of nobility. Badly washed-out.*

Color: *Badly overshot bite.*

Faults: *Doggy bitches. Poorly carried ears. Too fine heads. Weak muzzles. Improper muscular condition. Faulty coat, other than temporary condition. Badly affected teeth.*

Minor Faults: *Too coarse heads, Hooked tails. Too light, round or protuding eyes. Discolored teeth. Condition of coat, due to season or keeping.*

MADELEINE PICKUP

English and Irish Champion El Halcon of Brittas, illustrating top construction and quality.

THE BRITISH STANDARD*

Characteristics: *The characteristic expression of the German Shepherd gives the impression of perpetual vigilance, fidelity,* liveliness and watchfulness, alert to every sight and sound, with nothing escaping attention; fearless, but with decided suspiciousness of strangers — as opposed to the immediate friendliness of some breeds. The German Shepherd possesses highly developed senses, mentally and temperamentally. He should be strongly individualistic and possess a high standard of intelligence. Three of the most outstanding traits are incorruptibility, discernment and ability to reason.

General Appearance: The general appearance of the German Shepherd is a well-proportioned dog showing great suppleness of limb, neither massive nor heavy, but at the same time free from any suggestion of weediness. It must not approach the Greyhound type. The body is rather long, strongly boned, with plenty of muscle, obviously capable of endurance and speed and of quick and sudden movement. The gait should be supple, smooth and longreaching, carrying the body along with a minimum of up-and-down movement, entirely free from stiltiness.

Head and Skull: The head is proportionate to the size of the body; long, lean, and clean-cut, broad at the back of the skull but without coarseness, tapering to the nose with only a slight stop between the eyes. The skull is slightly domed and the top of the nose should be parallel to the forehead. The cheeks must not be full or in any way prominent and the whole head, when viewed from the top, should be much in the form of a V, well filled in under the eyes. There should be plenty of substance in foreface, with a good depth from top to bottom. The muzzle is strong and long and, while tapering to the nose, it must not be carried to such an extreme as to give the appearance of being overshot. It must not show any weakness, or be snipy or lippy. The lips must be tight fitting and clean. The nose must be black.

Eyes: The eyes are almond-shaped as nearly as possible matching the surrounding coat but darker rather than lighter in shade and placed to look straight forward. They must not be in any way bulging or prominent, and must show a lively, alert and highly intelligent expression.

Ears: The ears should be of moderate size, but rather large than small, broad at the base and pointed at the tips, placed rather high on the skull and carried erect — all adding to the alert expression of the dog as a whole. (It should be noted, in case *novice breeders may be misled, that in puppies the ears often hang until the age of six months and sometimes longer, becoming erect with the replacement of the milk teeth.)*

Mouth: *The mouth should be sound and strong, gripping with a scissor-like action, the lower incisors just behind, but touching the upper.*

Neck: The neck should be strong, fairly long with plenty of muscle, fitting gracefully into the body, joining the head with sharp angles and free from throatiness.

Forequarters: *The shoulders should slope well back. The ideal being that a line drawn through the center of the shoulder blade should form a right-angle with the humerous when the leg is perpendicular to the ground in stance. Upright shoulders are a major fault. They should show plenty of muscle, which is distinct from, and must not be confused with, coarse or loaded bone, which is a fault. The shoulder bone should be clean. The forelegs should be perfectly straight viewed from the front, but the pasterns should show a slight angle with the forearm when regarded from the side: too great an angle denotes weakness, and while carrying plenty of bone it should be of good quality. Anything approaching the massive bone of the Newfoundland, for example, is a decided fault.*

Body: *The body is muscular, the back is broadish and straight, strongly bone and well developed. The belly shows a waist without being tucked up. There should be a good depth of brisket or chest, the latter should not be too broad. The sides are flat compared to some breeds, and while the dog must not be barrel ribbed, it must not be so flat as to be actually slabsided. The German Shepherd must be quick in movement and speedy but not like a Greyhound in body.*

Hindquarters: *The hindquarters should show breadth and strength, the loins being broad and strong; the rump rather long and sloping and the legs, when viewed from behind must be quite straight, without any tendency to cow-hocks, or bow-hocks, which are both extremely serious faults. The stifles are well turned and the hocks strong and well let down. The ability to turn quickly is a necessary asset to the German Shepherd, and this can only be if there is good lenght of thigh-bone and leg, and by the bending of the hock.*

Feet: *The feet should be round, the toes strong, slightly arched* and held close together. The pads should be firm, the nails short and strong. Dew-claws are neither a fault nor a virtue, but should be removed from the hindlegs at 4 to 5 days old, as they are liable to spoil the gait.

Tail: When at rest the tail should hang in a slight curve, and reach at least as far as the hock. During movement and excitement it will be raised, but in no circumstances should the tail be carried past a vertical line drawn through the root.

Coat: The coat is smooth, but it is at the same time a double coat. The under-coat is wooly in texture, thick and close and to it the animal owes its characteristic resistance to cold. The outer-coat is also close, each hair straight, hard, and lying flat, so that it is rain-resisting. Under the body to behind the legs, the coat is longer and forms near the thigh a mild form of breeching. On the head (including the inside of the ears), to the front of the legs and feet, the hair is short. Along the neck it is longer and thicker, and in winter approaches a form of ruff. A coat either too long or too short is a fault. As an average, the hairs on the back should be from one to two inches in length.

Color: The color of the German Shepherd in itself is not important and has no effect on the character of the dog or on its fitness for work and should be a secondary consideration for that reason. All white or near white unless possessing black points are not desirable. The final color of a young dog can only be ascertained when the outer coat has developed.

Weight and Size: The ideal height (measured to the highest point of the shoulder) is 22-24 inches for bitches and 24-26 inches for dogs. The proportion of length to height may vary between 10:9 and 10:8.5.

Faults: A long, narrow, Collie or Borzoi head. A pink or livercolored nose. Undershot or overshot mouth. Tail with curl or pronounced hook. The lack of heavy undercoat.

THE GERMAN STANDARD

General Appearance: The German Shepherd Dog is a somewhat more than medium-sized dog. The average height at the back is 24 inches and should be checked with a measuring stick at the withers, with the coat pressed down and the stick touching the elbow and perpendicular from withers to ground. The correct

This is a champion Shepherd photographed at a show in Germany. The German Standard says, "A true to type German Shepherd Dog gives an impression of innate strength, intelligence and nimbleness, with harmonious proportions and nothing overdone or lacking. His whole manner of behavior should make it perfectly clear that he is sound in mind and body, and with the physical attributes to make him always ready for tireless action as a working dog."

heights for the German Shepherd Dog as a working breed are 60-65 cm (24 to 26 inches) for dogs and 55-60 cm (22-24 inches) for bitches. Anything outside these limits detracts from the suitability of the animal for working or breeding purposes. The German Shepherd Dog's body is slightly long in comparison to its height, and it is powerful and well muscled. The bone is dry and the frame well knit. The proportion between height and length, and the position and symmetry of the limbs (angulation) are so inter-related as to insure a long-reaching, tireless trotting gait. The coat is weather resistant. A pleasing appearance is desirable, but not at the price of putting the dog's suitability for work in any doubt. Sexual characteristics must be well defined:

The German Standard requires the German Shepherd to have the courage and determination to defend himself and his handler or his handler's property, should the need arise. He must go readily into the attack at his handler's command; but above all he must be an alert and pleasant member of his household, sure of his surroundings and devoted to them — in particular, gentle with children and other animals.

there should be no room for doubt that the dog is male and the bitch female.

A true-to-type German Shepherd Dog gives an impression of innate strength, intelligence and nimbleness, with harmonious proportions and nothing overdone or lacking. His whole manner and behavior should make it perfectly clear that he is sound in mind and body, and with the physical attributes to make him always ready for tireless action as a working dog. He must have an abundance of temperament, so that he can adapt himself to any situation and carry out any task given to him willingly and with pleasure. He must have the courage and determination to defend himself, his handler or his handler's property, should the need arise. He must go readily into the attack at his handler's command; but above all he must be an alert and pleasant member of his household, sure of his surroundings and devoted to them — in particular gentle with children and other animals — and at his ease in his dealings with other people: in short, a harmonious blend of innate nobility and alertness based on self confidence.

Angulation and Movement: *The German Shepherd is a trotting dog. His sequence of step therefore follows a diagonal pattern— the fore and hind leg on the same side always move in opposing directions. Therefore, his limbs must be so set in relation to each other — must have such angulation — that he can thrust the hind foot well up to the midpoint of the body, and have an equally long reach with the forefoot, without any appreciable alternation in the line of the back. The correct proportions of height to length with corresponding length of limbs will produce a groundcovering stride that travels flat over the ground giving an impression of effortless progression. With his head thrust forward and his tail slightly raised, a balanced and steady trotter displays a line running unbroken in a gentle curve from the tip of the ears over the neck and back to the tip of the tail.*

Nature and Character: *Strong nerves, alertness, calmness, watchfulness, loyalty and incorruptibility, courage, boldness and keenness are the outstanding characteristics of the purebred German Shepherd Dog. They make him a first-class working dog in any capacity, especially as a watch-dog companion or guard, or for police and herding duties.*

This Shepherd, photographed in Germany by Marianne von der Lancken, typifies the true Shepherd head according to the German Standard. It is proportionate in size to the body and without coarseness. In general, clean cut and fairly broad between the ears. The forehead is only slightly domed, whether viewed from front or side.

The Head: *The head should be proportionate in size to the body and without coarseness. In general clean cut and fairly broad between the ears. The Forehead is only slightly domed, whether viewed from front or side. A center furrow if present should be only shallow. The Cheeks should taper off laterally in a gentle curve without any forward protuberance. Viewed from above the Skull extends from the ears to the bridge of the nose, tapering gradually and evenly, and blending without any marked "stop" into the wedge-shaped, powerful muzzle. The Lips should be firm, dry, closing tightly and without any flews. The Bridge of the Nose is straight and almost parallel to the forehead. The Bite is strong, with the incisor teeth closing with a tight scissor action: an undershot bite is even more a fault than an overshot one. The Ears are of medium size, broad at the base and set well up. They taper to a point and are held pricked and slanting forward. Tipped ears are undesirable, and ears that drop or have been docked must be rejected. Puppies normally have their ears down until between the fourth and sixth months — sometimes even longer.*

The Eyes: *The Eyes are of medium size, almond shaped, set somewhat aslant and not protuberant. They should be as dark as possible, and give the impression of lively intelligence.*

The Neck: *The neck is powerful, well muscled, of medium length and with no loose folds or dewlap. It is raised up when excited but normally held level.*

The Body: *The chest is deep but not too broad, the ribs neither flat nor barrelled, the belly slightly drawn-up, the back and loins straight and well muscled, not too long from withers to croup. The length of the body should exceed the height at shoulder; square or "leggy" dogs should be rejected. The loins are broad and powerful, and the croup long and sloping gently down.*

The Tail: *The tail is bushy haired, must reach to the hock at least, and sometimes forms a hook to one side at the tip, though this is undesirable. The tail is normally carried falling in a gentle curve; but the curve tightens and the tail is carried higher when the dog is excited or in motion, although it should never pass the vertical. It should never, therefore, whether straight or curved, lie over the back. Docked tails should be rejected.*

Front Assembly: *The shoulder blade is long and set obliquely, lying flat against the body and not set forward. The upper arm*

The German Standard recognizes a Long Haired German Shepherd Dog, as seen here. Breeders refer to it as a "Scottish Shaferhund," meaning Scottish Shepherd dog, and voice a belief that at one time there was an infusion of Scotch Collie into the German Shepherd

should form a near right-angle to it, and like it should be well muscled. The foreleg should appear straight from all sides. The pasterns should be firm and not too steep, and the elbows should be turned neither in nor out.

Hind Assembly: The haunch is broad and well muscled. The upper thigh is fairly long, and viewed from the side is set diagonally to a proportionately long stifle bone. The stifle joint and hock are firm and powerful.

The Paws: The paws are short, rounded, well-knit and arched, with short, strong, preferably dark-colored nails. Dew-claws sometimes appear on the hind feet; as they cause the dog to go wide and can mar the gait, they should be removed soon after whelping.

Color: The color can be black, iron-gray, or ash-gray either as the solid color or with regular brown, tan or light gray markings, and sometimes a black saddle. Also dark sable — black overlay on a gray or light brown ground, with lighter markings to tone (the so-called "wolf color" — the original color of the wild dog). Small white markings on the forechest are permissible. The undercoat, except in the case of black dogs, is always of a lighter shade. The final color of a puppy cannot be determined until the guard hairs come through.

Coat: (a) The normal-haired German Shepherd Dog. The outer coat should be as thick as possible, made up of straight, coarse close-lying hairs, which are short on the head (including the inside of the ears) and the front of the legs, paws and toes, but longer and more profuse on the neck. The hair grows longer on the back of the legs, as far down as the pastern and the stifle, and forms fairly thick trousers on the quarters. There is no hard and fast rule for the length of the hair, but short, moletype coats are faulty.

(b) The long-haired German Shepherd Dog. The hairs are longer, not always straight, and definitely not lying close and flat to the body. They are distinctly longer inside and behind the ears, and on the back of the forearm and usually at the loins, and form moderate tufts in the ears and feathering from elbow to pastern. The trousers are long and thick. The tail is bushy with light feathering underneath. As this type of coat is not so weatherproof as the normal coat it is undesirable; but if there is sufficient undercoat it may be passed for breeding.

(c) The Long Open-coated German Shepherd Dog. The hair is appreciably longer than in (b), and tends to form a parting, particularly along the back. If present at all, the undercoat will be found only at the loins. Dogs with this type of coat are commonly narrow-chested, with narrow, overlong muzzles. As the long coat seriously diminishes the dog's protection from the weather and its general fitness for work, it should not be passed for breeding.

Faults: All of which exclude a dog from use for breeding. Any deficiency which detracts from a dog's working powers, stamina or performance, in particular lack of sex characteristics or of shepherd instinct, such as apathy, weak nerves, excitability, shyness, absence of one or of both testicles (both these faults bar a dog from breed survey or from classification at a show), *listlessness or disinclination to work, soft or flabby constitution or poor substance, Marked color-paling. Full albinos — that is dogs lacking all pigmentation and with pink noses, etc., and whiteish dogs — with near-white coats but black noses — are alike to be firmly excluded from breed survey and classification. Other faults are shoulder heights outside the prescribed limits; stunted growth; disproportionate height or length; weedy or coarse build; soft back; steep-set limbs or anything else that detracts from the reach or endurance of the gait; a muzzle that is too short, blunt, weak, pointed, overlong or lacking in strength; an over or under-shot bite, or any other fault in dentition, such as weak or worn-out teeth; a coat that is too short, too long, too soft or lacking in undercoat; drop ears or permanently faulty ear carriage; a tail that is too short, ringed or curled, or in general badly-set; docked ears or tail; a tail stumpy from birth.*

Champion Pull Wikingerblut SchH I. The suffix stands for the training degree *Schützhund* (see Appendix). In 1965 he was Best of Winners at the Chicago National Amphitheater — imported from Erich Sanders, Germany. Pull has an outstanding, ground-covering gait; strong head, good pigment, good shoulder angulation, good rear angulation and a strong back.

Wherever one travels in this world one meets the German Shepherd Dog at work; and it is no gimmick or idle boast to call him the greatest service dog in existence. Here we see one training at the police school outside of London.

III History of the German Shepherd Dog

Wherever one travels in this world one meets the German Shepherd Dog at work; and it is no gimmick or idle boast to call him the greatest service dog in existence. The jealous may belittle him, the ignorant may call him a wolf, and people who have never owned or even know a Shepherd will vie with each other in telling stories of his " treachery," but despite all this, he remains the undisputed " King" of the working breeds.

He is known as a messenger or Red Cross dog with the Army; a formidable addition to the police forces: tracker, guardian, defender of property; an avalanche dog in the mountainous districts of Europe; the guardian of valuable racehorses; farm worker; and, perhaps best of all, as a clever, trained actor in films and television.

All these have earned him a place of ever increasing importance in our modern way of living. So it is that wherever he is found, whatever his color or conformation, you will find that he inspires a deep affection and respect in the heart of his owner for the many qualities he possesses and for the sense of security he gives by reason of his vigilance. Last, but by no means least, he is important because of the pleasure his beauty gives, his noble head and expression, his harmony of physique and strength and grace of movement.

We know that the German Shepherd Dog was evolved from the

We know that the German Shepherd Dog was evolved from the ancient herding dogs of the provinces of Wurttemberg, Thuringia and the adjacent districts of Central Europe. This herding tradition has been passed on to our present-day German Shepherd.

ancient herding dogs of the provinces of Wurttemberg, Thuringia and adjacent areas of Central Europe. Here, over the centuries, the clearance of the heavily wooded areas and the advance in stockbreeding and agriculture created a need for an agile dog capable of moving swiftly after the wandering herds and flocks to prevent them from straying onto the crops in the fields and to protect them from depredations of man or wild beast.

The development of the German Shepherd Dog proper began just before the end of the 19th Century. It was in 1899, actually, that the *Verein Für Deutsche Schäferhunde* (often abbreviated SV) was founded in an effort to establish a selective breeding program for the improvement of the breed. The entire basis of the breed development in the early days consisted of selection for working qualities and was based on the dogs' skilful work with herdsmen and farmers in both fold and field. These are, in fact, qualities which we admire and respect today, and which every serious minded breeder is seeking to retain and consolidate, as opposed to the mere physical appearance of an attractive show ring specimen.

Although 1899 is generally considered the founding date for our

AKE WINTZELL

The entire basis of the breed development in the early days consisted of selection for working qualities. These are, in fact, qualities which we admire and respect today, and which every serious minded breeder is seeking to retain and consolidate as opposed to the mere physical appearance of an attractive show ring specimen.

breed, its history goes back much further. Guard and herd dogs, valued for their usefulness to man, were the earliest domesticated dogs, all of today's breeds having been developed from these ancestral types. The sheepherding dogs have remained relatively unchanged for thousands of years, modifying only in response to the varying requirements of their environments.

The Roman legions, lacking the means of refrigeration, were accompanied by trains of live sheep and cattle. In those days the only way to keep meat from spoiling was to keep it alive. Attending these trains were the herd dogs, and many of them remained in the wake of the Roman passage. The pasture lands in the German provinces of Saxony, Wurttemberg and Thuringia became the home of their descendants. The farmer worked hard for a living, and had a no-nonsense outlook on life. The dog either worked properly or it wasn't worth feeding. Thus selection and breeding were done solely on the basis of usefulness, no attention being paid to beauty. Because there is a " mean" build best adapted to the herding function, a general type was maintained although not deliberately.

Rittmeister (cavalry captain) Max Emil Friedrich von Stephanitz recognized the potential beauty and usefulness of the native sheepherding breeds and together with Artur Meyer founded the *Verein für Deutsche Schäferhunde* or Club for German Shepherd Dogs previously mentioned.

Ever since, through two wars, depression and occupation, this organization has controlled the destiny of the German Shepherd in its country of origin. Von Stephanitz died in 1936, but not before he lived to see the organization become solidly established — setting standards, licensing and regulating shows and even deciding which dogs were suitable for breeding. Yes, even that! Undoubtedly one reason for the high quality of the German Shepherd in Germany is that before a dog can be used for breeding he must be examined and certified by a representative of the SV. Otherwise the litter cannot be registered.

The fame of this superior guard dog soon spread to countries far away from the land of his origin. Early in the 20th Century the " Shepherd," as he is now known, came to America.

In Great Britain, his progress was slow and just when fanciers were making some headway, the First World War began and anti-German feeling ran high — even the inoffensive Dachshund was nearly eradicated — so that the development of the breed in the British Isles

After a great deal of deliberation and testing, the German Shepherd was selected as the breed most suitable for training as a guide to the blind. He is used for this purpose throughout the world, and from this has come his popular name, "The Seeing Eye Dog."

slowed almost to a halt. Members of the British Army serving on the Continent were much impressed by the dog's versatility as a messenger dog and guard, and at the close of hostilities many good dogs of the breed found their way back with the returning soldiers. They were originally classed by the English Kennel Club as Foreign Sheepdogs and afterwards as Alsatian Wolfdogs until the 1930s. Then they became merely Alsatians, until the title was eventually extended to "Alsatian (German Shepherd Dog)" which is a long and misleading appellation. Nobody really knows why "Alsatian" was chosen. When Alsace was part of Germany there were very few Shepherd dogs to be found there. Naturally the German breeders were — and are — displeased and confused by the misnomer.

However, the main cause of the breed's initial lack of popularity was the use of the name Wolfdog, since the majority of specimens seen in England in the early days were wolf-gray in color. This misconception helped to fan the flames of some fierce argument about the Shepherd's problematical descent, with accompanying stories about its "treacherous" behavior arising from untrue and derogatory gossip. All this, of course, rendered the entire breed, and the British specimens in particular, a great disservice. It is the fervent hope of the writer (and of a larger number of British breeders than is generally supposed) that the name "Alsatian" will eventually be dropped, and that the dog in Great Britain will then be known as it is in the rest of the world.

Konrad Lorenz, in his book, "King Solomon's Ring," gives one explanation of the origin of the breed. He tells how most large breeds of dog in Europe, including Great Danes and Wolfhounds, are pure "*aureus*" (i.e., descendants of the jackal) and contain, at the most, only a minute amount of wolf blood in their veins. However, very few students agree with him. Most believe that dogs are descendants of the wolf. However, if Lorenz is right then the strongly individualistic character of the German Shepherd springs from the independent

"Rufus," a member of the Atomic Energy Authority Constabulary at Aldemaster, England. These dogs, which guard the highly secret atomic energy installations, must undergo rigorous training to qualify for their job. Photo courtesy of Atomic Energy Authority Constabulary (by permission of Chief Inspector).

nature of the jackal *(canis aureus)*, which is a lone hunter confining its activities to a restricted area, while the Spitz breeds such as the Elkhounds, Samoyeds, Finsk Spets (Finnish Spitz), hunt in packs roaming far and wide, and live their lives bound up in their own pack. From an entirely different viewpoint, one could consider the term Wolfdog as anything but a stigma since one of the Shepherd dog's first acts of service and friendship to man was to protect him and his herds from marauding wolves. In this sense, "Wolfdog" is really a compliment to our dog.

Moreover, those who really know wolves, consider them one of the most wonderful of all the creatures of nature. Most of the stories concerning wolves' treachery and ferocity are just that — stories. There is no documented evidence to support them.

What we do know is that wolves are loyal, mating for life, and that both parents cooperate in rearing the young. For years there was a standing reward offered for proof of a wolf attack on a human. That reward was never collected.

So whether our German Shepherd descended from a jackal or, as is more likely, from a wolf, we have no need for apologies.

Around the World with the German Shepherd

All German Shepherd Dog breeders take pride in the breed's leading position as a service dog, and it is interesting to see how adaptable the Shepherd is to his varied work in all kinds of climates, in the many countries throughout the world where he is now established. It is equally of interest to know that there are flourishing and influential German Shepherd clubs and societies in almost every country, where training and breeding are encouraged and supervised, and where shows and matches are held to help the breeders in their efforts to obtain typical specimens.

Germany

In Germany, the numbers and quality of the best dogs surpass all other countries. This, of course, is only to be expected in the land where the Shepherd originated, and where he is bred under close supervision with all rules adapted to his individual development. The *Verein für Deutsche Schäferhunde* (S.V.), the parent of all our clubs, has great authority over the breed, and it is run in a thorough and serious manner which has no equal elsewhere. The membership for 1966 was almost 42,000; the entry at the *Sieger Hauptzuchtschau* was 650 exhibits, with 170 entries in the Open Dog Class alone. This gives an idea of the popularity of the breed in Germany where, on an average, over 5,000 litters are registered each year, plus, of course many unregistered dogs which are kept for work or as pets. The President's annual report is always a piece of plain speaking regarding the state of the breed, with warnings about any undesirable trends which may be developing and with praise for improvement. A list of dogs that have failed to pass the breed survey, as well as those who have qualified is also published, month by month, in the club journal. So, all in all, German breeders can see where they are going. Without doubt this highly perfected system of checking and controlling does much towards helping S.V. members to produce some very superior stock.

MADELEINE PICKUP

The Sieger Show, as seen here, is a mecca of all German Shepherdites, and some 40 nationalities are welcomed each year.

The *Siegerschau* is the Mecca of all German Shepherdites, and some forty nationalities are welcomed there each year. A great number of important sales are made at this show; buyers are keen, often paying very high prices for outstanding dogs or those carrying important bloodlines. Many of these dogs are exported, the chief buyers being the USA and Japan, while some find their way to the

Scandinavian countries and over the frontiers to Holland, Belgium and France. Great Britain also imports some good dogs from Germany, and a number go to the colonies. One thing which often surprises the newcomer is to see adult dogs, five or six years old, sold overseas. The reason is that a really top winner is not granted an export permit until he has sired enough litters to continue his line, so that the carefully balanced breeding program of the S.V. shall not be interrupted or disorganized by the loss overseas of an important animal before he has been used sufficiently.

France

France has a great number of top class German Shepherd Dogs; the breed is much more popular than generally supposed in that country where vast agricultural areas and mountainous frontiers call for useful working dogs. The French breeders are fortunate in being able to exhibit at the German *Siegerschau*. Some of their dogs have been placed in the *auslese* group here. The National Club's title is *La Société du Chien Berger Allemand*, and a well-produced quarterly magazine is published with really good pictures and show reports. The National Show, held annually at Vichy, is judged either by the President of the Club or by an S.V. judge from Germany, and the dogs are graded Excellent, Very Good, Good, and Unsatisfactory, in the German manner.

In common with most European countries, France has several mountainous frontier regions. Here the German Shepherd really comes into his own working with the frontier guards and customs officers on a number of jobs such as tracking escaping criminals and those engaged in smuggling activities. These dogs work in extreme temperatures at high altitudes; this calls for great stamina and courage. The stories of their resourceful conduct and bravery would fill a large book, and the dogs enjoy the respect of all who use the mountain passes.

On a visit to the lovely island of Corsica, we were surprised to see several excellent specimens of the breed working sheep, and also some being used as gun dogs. It appears that the island was occupied by German armed forces during the last war and when they withdrew, the dogs were left behind on the island where an appreciative Corsican peasantry was quick to realize their value as a utility animal.

Belgium and Holland

Belgium has a flourishing National Club, the *Royal Club du Berger Allemand de Belgique* which holds a well supported show each year, again with the advantage of an international entry which leads to great interest. The *Royal* awards the title of Prince and Princess to the winners of the young dog and young bitch classes, and those of King and Queen to those of the two open classes.

In the rural districts of Belgium, one can still see small carts laden with market produce and even milk being drawn by dogs. These are often German Shepherds, although there is some preference for their indigenous cousins, the Malinois Belge, and, occasionally, the strong and willing Groenendaal, another herding breed of similar appearance and character.

Holland is a country of working dogs where the German Shepherd naturally has a firmly established place. The Dutch keep closely in touch with the S.V. and attend the *Siegerschau* in large numbers. They favor the working type of dryfleshed animal with keen, even sharp intelligence, and have exported some excellent dogs.

Switzerland

Switzerland has the highest proportion of police dogs in relation to manpower — a ratio of one dog to every three policemen on the beat in the towns, and one dog to every man in the rural areas. In the small but difficult terrain of this lovely country, distances by road are great between villages and towns which are relatively close as the crow flies. It was here that the German Shepherd Dog specialized as a trusty messenger and precious liaison officer during the Swiss Army maneuvers. Indeed, they did so in earnest when warfare raged along Switzerland's frontiers in World War II. The number of training clubs in Switzerland is astonishing. On every Sunday morning one can see the dogs being put through their paces in almost every small community. In the towns they can be seen in the parks which are willingly conceded to the clubs since the Army and the police get their dogs from the breeders who are encouraged to produce suitable material for them.

Throughout the entire Alpine region, which extends beyond Switzerland's frontiers into Italy, Austria, Germany and parts of France, the German Shepherd is the king of the avalanche rescue

German Shepherds work with the police all over the world. Here is one on duty in West Germany. Switzerland has the highest proportion of police dogs in relation to manpower — a ratio of one dog to every three policemen on the beat in the towns, and one dog to every man in the rural areas.

dogs, replacing the traditional Saint Bernards. It would be impossible to count the human lives saved by their splendid courage and extraordinary flair for finding buried persons when disaster has struck. The acute hearing and instinct of the rescue dogs astounds even the seasoned handler; stories of their heroism in the bitter cold and deep treacherous snow after the avalanches are recounted with pride by all who work with them.

The lonely herdsman or shepherd tending his animals, which are taken high up the steep mountains to graze during long weeks in the summer, uses his dog as a mailman. He is dependent on him, too, for contact with his home and sometimes even for provisions which the dog faithfully carries attached to a harness on his back, up the rugged mountain slopes from the farm in the valley far below.

The Swiss International Championship Show is held in these beautiful surroundings at Lucerne. Here is the lineup of German Shepherds in the huge ring.

Before judging is completed, the dogs' pedigrees must be examined. Swiss International Champion Show at Lucerne.

At Lucerne, Switzerland the dogs are benched indoors in a beautifully clean and impressive display.

Swiss International Canine Exhibitions are held annually, in a different area each year. All the large towns take their turn in being host to the show which attracts entries and visitors from all over Europe. The German Shepherd is always accorded first class facilities, with a tremendous ring where the dogs are examined and graded as in Germany. Some beautiful dogs have been bred by the Swiss; several have found their way to America and Canada.

The German Shepherd is very much a family dog in Switzerland, and in the outlying districts he can often be seen accompanying the children to school; afterwards returning to the homestead and then going back, always punctually, to fetch his young charges home again when school is over.

Scandinavia

Sandinavia has a large German Shepherd population; here again he is prized as a police dog. Many good dogs are imported into the three countries from Germany. The quarantine is long; in Sweden all dogs have to have an examination for hip dysplasia, with their radiographs passed by the authorities before entry is granted. In addition, a blood test for Leptospirosis is made when the dog arrives in Sweden where the possibility that this contagious disease might be introduced is dreaded by the mink farmers in particular.

Sweden has a corps of German Shepherds specially trained for avalanche rescue work. Helicopters carry the rescuers and their dogs to the scene of the snow slide which in Scandinavia can be enormous. Should landing conditions be too difficult, animals and men parachute down and the dogs search for survivors. Then, if the helicopters still cannot come in, the dogs are used to draw the survivors out on sleds.

In Sweden, where heavy avalanches are common, there is a corps of German Shepherds especially trained for avalanche rescue work.

AKE WINTZELL

Delivered by helicopter, or dropped by parachute, this well trained Shepherd uses his keen sense of smell to search for possible victims buried under the snow.

With the victim located, his barking will bring rescuers to the scene.

Should conditions be too difficult for aircraft to land, the dogs are hitched to an air-dropped sled and they pull the injured person to safety.

Czechoslovakia

Czechoslovakia has always been a country of German Shepherd enthusiasts, and in the days before the 1939 war Czechs bought dogs extensively at the famed *Siegerschau* in Germany. When the first International Canine Exhibition was held in Prague a few years ago, there were touching scenes when breeders met each other again after the long years of war and post war disruption. There was great joy at finding that a large number of valuable lines had been preserved through those difficult times.

Russia does not give many details of her canine population, but we know that our breed is used widely with the Army there and also as a guard dog in prison camps. There are few shows which foreigners may attend, and no private kennel clubs as we know them, so our assumption is that breeding is state controlled.

Africa

Egypt's police use Shepherds in many branches of their work. We sent them a bitch, chosen by the chief of police, some years ago. She was used for detecting cholera. This disease is waterborne and has a distinct odor, so the bitch was trained to detect it and give warning of its presence in the river — an unusual task for our talented breed.

Nearly all of the African countries have German Shepherds, mostly acquired from Great Britain. Many of the native policemen, particularly in Nigeria, have been trained at the Metropolitan Police Dog Training Establishment near London, afterwards returning home with their dogs to take up their duties and instruct others. The dogs acclimatize quite well, although their coats usually become somewhat sparse due to the hot humid climate, and they are treated with affection and great consideration for their valued work with their handlers in troubled spots. Kenya, Rhodesia and most southern African countries have flourishing breed and training clubs; the South African Kennel Union fosters showing activities, and some beautifully organized shows are held throughout these lovely countries.

Famous diamond mines, such as De Beers, have a canine police force of their own. The gold mines, too, use them in considerable numbers for security work. The large estates where coffee is grown make an ideal setting for the German Shepherd in his role of companion-guard to the lonely farmer or planter. It is here that the dog's vigilance and protective instinct for his owner and family have saved many lives during local troubles.

Obedience work, taught at the training clubs, naturally helps to fit the dog for his work as a guardian. The standard of work is high, with great keenness among the handlers to produce a winner at their competitions.

South America

South America is steadily increasing her interest in the breed, particularly in Brazil where prizewinning animals are eagerly sought after by the breeders. Brazilians are great animal lovers, noted for their fine horses and skilled riders. They are sure to be successful with the German Shepherd. Their breed club is already a well-established concern, running excellent shows. As in South Africa, the breed provides guards for the large number of mines and plantations all over South America.

Japan

Japan has become very Shepherd-minded since the last war, and the Japanese come in large numbers to the Sieger Show each year, where they appear to be photographing every exhibit, so numerous are they, with still or movie cameras. High prices are paid by the Japanese for the top qualified dogs each year, and many good ones travel to the Orient after the show.

Japan has become very Shepherd-minded since the last war, and the Japanese come in large numbers to the Sieger Show in West Germany each year. High prices are paid, and many good dogs, such as this one, travel to the Orient after the show.

SALLY ANNE THOMPSON

Hawaii

Hawaii has a flourishing German Shepherd Dog Club in Honolulu where a championship show is held annually. This event attracts entries from all the islands in the group. When we judged there some years ago nearly 100 dogs were entered. There is a very fine training club in Honolulu, as there are on most of the other islands. We saw Shepherds guarding the houses and estates of many of the sugar and pineapple planters. The climate and conditions are ideal for the breed in this near Paradise.

Australia

Australia has a law forbidding the importation of Shepherds as it was found that when they mated with the dingoes (wild dogs), the offspring caused chaos in the extensive sheep-rearing areas. However, there still remain a few descendants of those sent out there many years ago but they differ a lot from our present day type, and are rather the "poor cousins" at the shows.

New Zealand, in contrast, is building up a very competitive group of well-bred dogs, mostly imported from Great Britain. They have splendid training classes for all branches of work, and some hotly contested conformation shows. The climate and territory are both ideal for the breed, which is fast gaining favor all over these islands.

Great Britain

Great Britain is very much the second home of the German Shepherd; there he tops the registrations at the English Kennel Club, with around 13.000 dogs registered each year. The police dog training is perhaps the most advanced in the world today, particularly in the Metropolitan (London) Force Establishment, where highly specialized training has been carried out for the detection of drug smuggling and many branches of detection work. The police trained dog has earned a wonderful and well-merited reputation for cooperation in countless arrests all over the country. Each force has its own trained dogs; these are individually developed according to the area they patrol, there being a wide difference between the work of the dog on a beat in town and one which roams with its handler in the forests and moors.

Police dog training in England is perhaps the most advanced in the world today, particularly in the metropolitan (London) force establishment. Here a dog is learning to scale a nine-foot wall.

The armed services also use the dogs in great number for patrol work, guarding camps, supplies and valuable equipment. The dog handlers are very attached to their charges, and they put on splendid displays at tournaments and shows all over the country to display their skill and intelligence.

A great number of breed and training clubs are active throughout the United Kingdom, and competition is extremely keen at all the Championship and Open Shows. Some 200 dogs are exported each year, mostly to the Commonwealth, where, according to the records they frequently make up as Champions. The Seeing Eye movement is well supported by the breed in Britain, and much good work is achieved which lends luster to the German Shepherd's good name. Dogs are also used in schools to teach road safety to children — another excellent job done by the breed.

United States and Canada

German Shepherds are very much a part of all canine activities in the United States and in Canada where they have been imported from Germany since before World War I. They are extensively used by the armed forces as sentry and guard dogs, and form an important part of the modern soldier's equipment. The German Shepherd Dog Club of America is a powerful body with subsidiaries across the country. These take turns as hosts to the National Specialty Show, an event which attracts huge entries of top class animals, the top winner of either sex gaining the title of either Grand Victor or Grand Victrix. The Club publishes a monthly magazine which is an exceptionally fine production. It has been named several times "the best canine magazine in the states," a title it richly deserves.

Training classes are held everywhere, and the competition in obedience work is keen. Some of Germany's best dogs find their way to the states, and from them many beautiful specimens are produced. The same can be said of Canada and, of course, many dogs cross the border both ways for showing and breeding purposes. The German Standard is closely followed. All North American judges are licensed by the American Kennel Club, so that a considerable amount of control is exercised, which benefits the breed.

The Seeing Eye movement is nationwide, and all American breeders take pride as pioneers in this most worthy cause. A large variety of breeds are used by the police; but the Shepherd is not the least of them by any means. In fact, he is used as a working dog much the same as in Europe, and enjoys a great reputation for his sagacity, his stamina and his appearance and reputation which strike terror into those bent on the commission of crime.

When choosing a puppy, the choice of color is a matter of personal choice. The ears of German Shepherd puppies, during the first few weeks or even the first few months of life, are down. As the dog matures and the muscles strengthen, they erect themselves. Frequently they will drop or "become soft" during teething. This is perfectly normal and no cause for concern.

IV Choosing Your German Shepherd

Before buying, remember that this breed needs ample exercise. It is both unwise and unfair to choose a dog that has been bred for generations to run tirelessly and then let him sit by the fireside or languish in a small apartment. His health and temperament will be sure to suffer from such confinement unless he gets plenty of outdoor exercise. And if he is chosen to be a guard dog he should be exercised and given as much freedom as possible when off duty.

Male or Female?

The bitch's adaptable nature and the ease with which she can be housebroken make her the ideal home companion. To the inquiry of whether or not she is the best choice for a family with children I would answer yes — if the children are suitable companions for *any* dog. In common with other breeds, however, she will soon grow tired of being teased and pulled about by small hands — hands that can also inflict discomfort, and even pain, to a young puppy.

We have had females in our own and in countless friends' families that have become loved and respected members of the household, tolerant, obedient, affectionate and ready to lay down their lives for

SALLY ANNE THOMPSON

The bitch's adaptable nature and the ease with which she can be housebroken make her the ideal home companion. The idea is to teach dog and child to live together in mutual consideration.

those around them. However, they do have a great sense of fairness and will, in the end, resent, as any dog will, being subjected to thoughtless pushing around. The ideal is to teach dog and child to live together in mutual consideration. Then you will have the ideal child's companion, and if the dog is chosen from a strain with sound nerves, no finer guardian could be found anywhere.

The bitch's mating seasons may be a drawback in a neighborhood where there are many dogs roaming about loose, or if the owner has no private, well-fenced area where the dog can be kept during her periods of heat. A bitch usually comes into her first heat at nine months to a year of age. Thereafter she can be expected to come into heat about every six months. The heat period can last up to 28 days although 21 is more usual. This is the only time that a female is willing to mate. When not in heat she rejects a male's advances. Present day deodorants will, to a great extent, prevent the broadcasting of her condition. Chlorophyll tablets can be given orally, and one of the many repellent atomizers may be utilized to spray her hindquarters and along doorways where dogs may sniff. These products are helpful but they do not change the bitch's instincts which are frequently in direct opposition to her owner's at these times. She is quite likely to find a way out to select a most unsuitable husband unless closely guarded during the danger period.

It is extremely cruel to shut up an animal who normally has plenty of freedom — even though she must be watched — and every effort should be made to give her some daily exercise. One way is to take her by car to a spot well away from home so that "suitors" cannot follow her trail back to your door. Another way around the problem is to look for a suitable boarding kennel and, once you are satisfied that she will have proper care, plus the security necessary, reserve her a kennel for these bi-annual "holidays." Once the regularity of her season is established, you will be able to anticipate her going into heat.

Except at these two periods a year a bitch's main interest is her owner and his family, and most bitches will make children or other small animals the object of their maternal care and concern. Their instincts are highly developed as guardians and they are usually very clean in their habits.

Of course, if you do not intend to breed your female, you can have her spayed. This is a routine minor operation which involves removing the ovaries. With these gone she will not go into heat, she will not be attractive to males, nor will she want to mate. The

Most bitches will make children or small animals the object of their maternal care and concern.

operation requires a minimum of hospitalization. It will not affect her personality. If she does get fat after spaying, it will not be because of the operation, but because she was overfed and under exercised.

If a German Shepherd bitch is given the exercise she should have, she will not become fat, spayed or whole.

A male (admitting that there are exceptions) is interested in a possible flirtation *all* the time. He may be equally devoted but he does not know that temptation is there to be resisted and may be found A.W.O.L. It is for this reason that females are usually chosen to be trained as Seeing Eye dogs, and this is worth remembering when choosing your new puppy.

Having made up your mind as to the sex and possibly the color you prefer, you can now go on to the actual selection of your new friend. If you have decided on a puppy with championship potential the choice will be more complicated so let us start with a discussion of the show puppy and deal with the companion dog later.

Selecting a Show Dog

In a breed like the German Shepherd, evolved from several strains of dogs including shepherds, there has been, as we have already mentioned, a considerable change in physique and size, so that an animal which won high honors in pre-war days would be less likely to do so now.

A potential exhibitor should not purchase in haste or he may well repent at leisure! Take time to study the standards of the breed and to visit several of the biggest championship shows in your area and note the winning dogs and their pedigrees. Approach the breeders or owners of the parents of any winning dog that particularly appeals to you. Try talking to as many people as possible in order to gather a cross section of opinion. Dog breeders are not, unfortunately, very generous in praise of kennels other than their own, so don't take just one opinion, consider several. Then, if you decide that a puppy by Champion X or out of Champion A is what you desire, get in touch with its owner and ask if there are litters by Champion X at nearby kennels which you can visit.

Choice of color is largely a personal affair. Many exhibitors maintain that a normal sable is never looked at in the ring while a flashy black and gold takes the eye of all judges. We are not of this opinion. The most important point to remember is that a German Shepherd to be considered for show must have good pigmentation with a dark mask, dark eyes and points as well as dark claws. Deep pigmentation in all colors is absolutely essential, and if a sable is chosen, watch this particularly — black points and the end of the guard hairs should be as dark as possible since color paling is an ugly fault and very difficult to breed out later on. What this means is that as a puppy matures, the area of light marking tends to widen so that a puppy which is predominantly black at the time of purchase may as an adult have only a black mask, saddle and possibly a few other limited areas of black, all the rest having become a lighter color.

The eyes should be dark in any case, but full of expression, not just dark "blanks."

Do not purchase a potential show puppy without having seen both parents. A strong strain on one side can stamp its type on puppies; but as the puppy matures, the undesirable faults from the other side may well appear and swamp the virtues.

Having decided on type, you will find yourself at the kennel eager

These two show dogs like to join the family fun.

to pick out your future winner. Ask if you may be allowed to handle the puppies and do so carefully. Puppies have a charming way of "choosing" their new owners, so make sure it is the one you truly desire if an adorable ball of fluff climbs up your legs and pleads to be adopted! Watch the puppies moving around and note if the movement is strong and even. All puppies are inclined to roll but the limbs should be straight and firm and their action quick and fleeting. Put your hand between the two front legs to feel if the sternum is firm and well developed; the "chest" should not feel hollow. Check that the "bite" is even, neither under — or overshot — a true bite just overlaps with the top teeth resting over the lower ones in the "scissor bite." A puppy's mouth may be slightly uneven but will become normal with maturity. It is wise to ask to see the parents' mouths if you are in doubt.

Health Check

Does he look well nourished? Are his nose and eyes mucousy?

Examine his teeth and gums: the teeth should be white and not pockmarked and the gums pink. Are his ears free from any sign of infection? Does his body feel firm and solid? Check his feet. His paws may seem too big but he'll grow up to them. Remember that a healthy dog is an extravert. He'll be bright-eyed, alert, and very much interested in you and everything that's going on around him. A shy pup may turn out to be satisfactory but the exuberant puppy is the better bet.

Take a look at the puppy's abdomen to see if the skin is firm and clear of any kind of rash or redness, and see if the hind dewclaws have been properly removed, if any were present at birth.

Many puppies do not have their ears erect before five or six months or even later. However, ears should start to move forward and show signs of lifting when the puppy is eight to ten weeks old.

Make inquiries about worm dosing—when it was done and with what vermifuge. We dose at five or six weeks and again at three months. However, it is best to find out what methods have been used in the puppy's home kennel. Get information about any inoculations already given, and a health guarantee.

Even a doughty German Shepherd knows when to quit.

Choosing a Pet

As for a pet puppy, follow the suggestions already given for choosing a healthy show specimen. It is heartbreaking, particularly when there are children, to lose a new pet through disease or unsoundness.

Every breeder will have some puppies that fall below show standard by reasons of uneven mouths, poor ear carriage, long or soft coats, less than perfect proportion, or of over or under size. None of these faults can possibly prevent one from enjoying all the fun and companionship of a true German Shepherd, but at a price far less than asked for a top show specimen. The pitfalls awaiting the pet dog buyer lie in the unsound or badly reared puppy, or one that has been involved in an accident in the kennel through careless handling or pure hazard.

We are not greatly in favor of the purchase of a cheap puppy advertised in the local newspapers. They are undoubtedly some reputable breeders advertising here but, in the main, the puppies advertised are the products of pet Shepherds reared by novices who, although kind and considerate, are without the knowledge and experience to raise a family of hearty feeders. A puppy badly weaned, or left too long on the dam without the supplementary diet so necessary to such a rapidly developing breed, is sure to give endless work and anxiety to the new owner, as well as cause considerable expense in veterinary advice and remedies.

Pet Shops

Many city dwellers do not have ready access to kennels, and for these people pet shops offer a convenient source for purchasing dogs. A larger pet shop will almost always have a number of specimens of a popular breed like the German Shepherd from which the prospective purchaser can make a selection. A reliable pet shop will, in addition, provide a written health guarantee which provides for approval of the dog by a veterinarian (within a reasonable time limit) before the sale becomes final.

A conveniently located pet shop is also advantageous in that it is a ready source of professional help and instruction during those first few weeks when untutored pup and amateur owner are learning to adjust to each other.

We maintain that a puppy cannot be sold with a year's guarantee

The "just a pet" buyer is free to choose a dog which appeals most to him without worrying about show points, nor must he have a dog of the "present-day" type.

like a good watch! But the purchaser can, by going to a recognized breeder or well-known pet shop, at least have the assurance of a well-bred, properly reared puppy, and be given the correct diet and some useful advice on the handling of his new baby. Nothing is so precious as a good start in life, and German Shepherd Dogs which are born weighing an average 16 ounces and must attain the normal 75 to 80 pounds by the time they are a year old, require enormous quantities of food.

We are often amused at visitors' exclamations over the large bowls of food being prepared for our German Shepherds at feeding time, but their comments also serve as a warning that novice owners are not usually aware of the ample dietary requirements of the breed.

So the "just a pet" buyer is really a free agent to choose the dog which appeals most to him. He is not restricted by show points, nor must he have a dog of the present-day type. Sometimes I find myself envying him. Longcoats and lop-ears always seem to have the nicest dispositions and pull terribly at one's heartstrings when they leave the kennel for a new home!

Be sure to ask for a full diet sheet before taking your puppy home; follow it carefully. It will make the transition much easier since he will continue eating familiar foods and not suffer an upset stomach.

You will, if the show ring is your aim, have already obtained a copy of the breed standard and any literature issued by your national breed club. Clubs are invariably glad to offer assistance to newcomers and to indicate branch clubs and training classes if requested to do so.

A dog does not, of course, have to conform to any beauty standard to be trained. Indeed, some of our best performers at obedience shows have been distinctly odd in appearance! All dogs are improved by training so do join an obedience training class if possible, and get the best out of your pet for his benefit as well as for your own.

Registration

Now that you have chosen your puppy, ask for the registration papers and the pedigree. The former may not yet be available as the kennel clubs are often behind with this branch of their work, and several weeks may elapse before the certificates are issued. However, you should get the pedigree with the date of birth and all details, and some breeders even offer a choice of names which gives added pleasure to the new owners. But if the puppy has already been registered by the breeder (or seller) you will also need a signed transfer and this should be requested at the time of purchase, even for a pet or companion dog as you may want the papers later should the animal turn out to be of show quality. Dog breeders sometimes move away so it is sometimes difficult to trace them after any lapse of time. Complete the deal formally at the time of purchase to avoid future problems.

Kindness and occasional tidbits will go a long way towards making your new puppy feel at home.

V   The First Six Months

Most puppies suffer from travel sickness during their first trip by car, and some for a few trips afterward until they become used to motion and the noise of a moving vehicle. When you go to pick up your new purchase take a large cardboard box with you, padded with a deep layer of shredded newspaper, and an old bath towel for the puppy to lie on. Also, a box of tissues in case of accidents. We like to give our pups a drink of honey and water a short time before starting out — a teaspoonful of honey to a cup of tepid water is usually satisfactory. This seems to soothe the stomach and nerves, but it is not infallible.

Give the kennel notice of the time of your arrival and request that the puppy not be fed beforehand. If a puppy is kept warm and out of drafts he will not suffer by missing a meal and he will be much more comfortable traveling on an empty stomach.

When you reach home try to restrain the family, particularly young children, as they will all want to caress and nurse the new arrival. But it is frightening and dangerous to allow any small animal to be overwhelmed by human attention even though kindly intended. Contrast his quiet regular existence in the kennel where he was probably one of a gang, with the sudden limelight of becoming a "star" in human company. How confusing and even terrifying it could be! It might easily give him a nervous temperament for life. So take it easy during his introduction to your home and, if at all possible, allow him to wander around and sniff at unfamiliar objects. He will answer his own questions with his nose and, given a little time, soon feel reassured in his new surroundings.

It is a good idea to anticipate all this by sending a small piece of old blanket or a burlap sack to his breeder and ask him to put it in the puppy's kennel so that it absorbs a familiar scent. Place this in his new bed and it will help him settle down in his new home.

He has probably been trained to perform his natural functions on newspapers, so some should be put down, either outdoors or in some quiet corner, and the puppy left to relieve himself as soon as possible after his arrival. Further on in this chapter we discuss indoor and outdoor housebreaking in detail.

The Bed

His first need is a suitable bed. It may not be the kind of bed you envision for a dog; but his health and often his behavior will depend on sleeping quarters. If he is to be kennelled, take care that no direct draft flows over his bed. One has only to watch how a dog curls up and puts his tail around his muzzle to protect himself from the cold draft when resting on the ground to realize how dogs fear a chilly current of air. We keep the dog beds in our kennel on legs about six inches from the floor and with a strong ledge about eight inches deep in front to hold back the bedding (wood shavings or straw, whichever you use). This ledge should have a metal strip (we use zinc) firmly nailed along it to prevent chewing. It is not only infuriating to see a new bed chewed up but extremely dangerous if the dogs swallow splinters or injure their mouths and gums on them.

If your puppy is to sleep indoors one of the many commercially manufactured beds such as those contructed of washable canvas with a metal folding frame are excellent. Put an old piece of blanket or some cozy woolen material on it, not forgetting the "smelly" piece brought from his old kennel. It is quite extraordinary how a young puppy will settle down if he has this little bit of comfort to turn to in a strange world full of unfamiliar objects.

If you prefer to wait until the puppy is older before buying him an expensive bed, you might like to do as we have frequently recommended to everyone's satisfaction: bed him down in an old tire placed on a square of plywood (see illustration) and comfortably filled with a blanket. This is proof against chewing as well as the much to be dreaded drafts

An old tire placed on a square of plywood may be pressed into service as a bed.

The puppy, having been introduced to his new sleeping quarters and his toilet arrangements, should now be given a warm drink of half milk and half water with a teaspoonful of honey dissolved in about 1/2 pint of the mixture. Do not attempt to feed him any solid food until he has made himself comfortable and drunk at least part of his milk. (Puppies who have not yet had cows' milk in their diet sometimes have difficulty with diarrhea. If symptoms appear discontinue the milk for a time and then introduce it very gradually into the diet.) A small meal of raw meat (unless he is accustomed to cooked or commercially packaged foods) can be given about an hour afterwards. Then leave him to rest with a large bone or a toy such as a thick rubber ring (we have never given a ball for a plaything since the time we nearly lost a dog when one lodged in his throat.)

The First Nights

It is wise to bring a new puppy home early in the day in order to get him used to his new surroundings before it is time for bed. He will naturally miss his warm littermates to curl up with and may well say so in a loud voice. Have ready a large beef bone. When his toilet arrangements have been seen to and his last feed given, put him on his bed and settle him firmly with more encouragement: "Good Kim, bed!" "Nice bed, Kim!", for instance, always emphasizing the word you wish to convey to him, along with his name and some praise. Later on, you will only have to say " Bed" and he will go there at once if you just show a little patience during his first week or so in your home.

Now give him the bone, and put his thick pile of newspaper beside the bed. It is unlikely that a young puppy will last the night without having to pass urine.

If he is noisy when left alone (and he is almost sure to be) return to him and settle him again on his bed, using the command again along with comforting words. Make sure he is not sleeping in a draft. If he goes over to lie against an outside door — which is something most puppies like to do — and the weather is cold, put an old mat or some other protection against the winds that blow under the door but on the opposite side so he cannot drag it away.

Puppy Feeding

The seller should have supplied you with the puppy's diet and feeding schedule, and you will have whatever is necessary ready for the new arrival. Try to follow the original schedule for a week at least, even if you disagree with it. It is sheer folly to take a puppy away from his familiar surroundings, his littermates, and sometimes his mother, and expect him to be happy when his stomach is upset by unfamiliar food fed at irregular intervals. If you wish to change the brand of meat or dog meal, or even the vitamin additives, do it gradually and watch his reactions carefully. We mentioned this earlier in connection with the addition of unaccustomed milk to his diet. The

A dog should learn at an early age to respect all members of the household, and this means animals as well as humans. Any tendency to attack or even behave obnoxiously should meet with a quick reprimand, and if necessary, punishment. Aggressive behavior cannot be tolerated in a family pet.

same response must be anticipated whenever strange foods are given although not as extreme as with milk. As the puppy matures his stomach will be less easily upset.

He may be teething too, and this can cause a digestive upheaval. He will chew and find unsuitable things to eat at such times, like coal and pebbles, wood, and of course, your rugs — the best ones, naturally. See that he is well supplied with chewable toys as well as a big bone when left alone and at bed time.

We are great believers in health foods and herbal remedies both for ourselves and for our dogs, and we hope you will want to use these natural foods and remedies as far as possible. They have given our kennel's dogs a widely recognized reputation for health and stamina. We have chosen a natural breed, a great outdoor breed, which thrives in natural surroundings. So let us feed our German Shepherds as naturally as today's circumstances will allow

You will have to rise early for the puppy's toilet needs, so we make no excuse for suggesting he be given his first meal at 7:30 am, and if you wish it, even earlier!

83

Lifting the Puppy

With so much carrying of the puppy, it is important to know how to lift him without damaging his tender limbs or frightening him by causing pain, something that can easily be done with such a heavy puppy. Most German Shepherds weigh from 25 to 30 pounds when nine weeks old. Never lift or allow a puppy to be lifted by the scruff of the neck. This is extremely painful and gives him the feeling of being choked. Restrain him by grasping the loose skin of the neck and slipping the other hand under his hindquarters. Grasp both his hocks and lift him "sitting" on your hand. You will then have perfect control and restraint and a comfortable puppy.

PRUDENCE WALKER

The correct way to hold a puppy.

Indoor Housebreaking

Housebreaking requires patience and watchful waiting on the part of the owner. So keep your eye on the new puppy constantly for the first few days. Unless he can be taken outdoors on short warning half a dozen times a day, he will have to be trained to use newspaper or a sand or litter box. (I recommend newspaper since it is easier to dispose of.)

The average puppy has five or six bowel movements every 24 hours and he will have to urinate even more often. Since he will want to pass a stool shortly after each feeding, within ten minutes after he has finished a meal place him on newspaper and keep him there until he has evacuated. It sometimes helps if a sheet of already soiled paper is kept with the clean as the odor will stimulate him to action. There are also housebreaking scents available at pet shops that serve this same purpose.

In the early stages, he should be kept in reasonably confined quarters. As soon as the puppy has relieved himself he may be allowed to play around the room, but not for long as he may be well want to relieve himself again. A young puppy should not be allowed the freedom of a whole house with a piece of newspaper in the corner of one room. He will quickly forget that it is there and perform his function wherever he happens to be. The paper should always be within seeing distance.

To repeat, watchful waiting is the keynote. It is much better to anticipate the act than to clean up after it. Generally, a puppy who is about to defecate will turn around and around several times before getting down to action. In the early months this behavior is the same in male and female. It is only when the male reaches puberty that he begins to cock a hind leg.

If you can catch the puppy just before he defecates, good! If he is on the paper where he should be, wait until he finishes before you praise him (and you should always praise him ardently). Otherwise he will undoubtedly come waddling toward you, leaving a watery trail behind.

If you catch him *not* using the paper, shame him and carry him to it. But never rub his nose in the mess. This hurts his dignity. Let him know by the tone of your voice how displeased you are. Praise when he uses the right place and shame when he does not, are two things to constantly keep in mind.

If you discover the evidence of a mishap some time after it has occurred, it is pointless to blame the puppy since he will not know what he is being scolded for. You will find that anticipation does far more good than correction.

Since puppies are loath to soil their beds, some trainers keep them in a very small enclosed box overnight (ventilated, of course) and then carry them from the box to newspaper or out of doors immediately upon rising.

Cleaning Up

The best way for coping with a puddle on the carpet is to squirt soda water from a syphon after mopping up the surplus liquid. This is an excellent way to keep new stains from forming, but it has little or no effect on old, dried stains. If there is no soda water, rub the area with soap and water to which has been added a little disinfectant, then dry thoroughly. If puddles are wiped up immediately they do not often leave stains, but small puppies can make large puddles, and a smell can accumulate. An air freshener spray is a useful and handy camouflage. If a mess becomes encrusted into a carpet, the spot can be washed with a special paste obtainable from most pet shops and drug stores. If the feces are completely dry, they can be brushed off with a strong wire brush, and vacuumed up. But it is far better to clean up immediately after an accident; otherwise the smell will attract the puppy back to the spot.

A puppy can be housebroken in two or three nights if one is prepared to make trips outside—perhaps three times the first night, twice the second night, and once for a couple of nights following if he is restless. It also depends on whether these nocturnal wanderings will be tolerated by the human members of your household.

Outdoor Housebreaking

If you are a homeowner with a back door opening onto a yard or garden, you can forego the paper training altogether, although the use of newspaper is a good habit for all puppies to acquire, so that in bad weather or illness, it can be resorted to.

When training a puppy to use the outdoors, follow much the same procedure as we have outlined above, but put him on the ground instead. Watch him until he has performed his function, then immediately bring him back inside while praising him highly. He will probably choose a spot the first time he is out, and it helps if you will then return him to that spot on later visits. This helps too, when it comes to raking up and burying the feces.

To teach a paper trained puppy to use the outdoors instead, gradually move the newspaper nearer and nearer to the door, then under the door with only a corner showing, and finally, weighted down with stones in the yard. If you live in an apartment, take a soiled paper with you the first few trips and spread it in the street.

When you walk the puppy on a leash, always follow the same route. He will soon show a preference for a certain spot. The leash should be long enough to give the dog freedom to sniff about and choose his spot. Since smells are important to a dog, don't pull the puppy away from a good "sniffy" spot unless it is obviously polluted.

When walking a dog (and a male in particular), you have certain obligations to the community. He should be taught to use the street, not the sidewalk, nor valuable shrubbery, automobile tires, store fronts and the like. It is a good idea to keep him in the gutter until he has completed his functions, and only then permit him on the sidewalk.

The adult dog, if fed only once a day, will require at least three walks a day: the first thing in the morning, shortly after his big meal, and just before bedtime. Two of these can be short but at least one should be for at least two miles.

Sometimes a well housebroken dog will deliberately show his displeasure when disciplined or left alone by leaving a puddle on the best rug or even on a sofa or bed. The only answer to such an act is extremely firm discipline. A scolding harangue accompanied by a good shaking or even a light switching with a rolled up sheet of newspaper should be delivered. The American training authority, the late Blanche Saunders, believed that many dogs who urinate deliberately do so for spite and that even the toughest punishment is wasted on them. They accept their discipline willingly for the satisfaction of "getting even."

Coprophagy

Another bad habit that some puppies pick up is eating their own stool if it is left with them. We are not sure of the cause but it may be related to a nutritional deficiency, and sometimes supplementing the diet with a vitamin mineral mixture ends the practice. In any event it stops when the dog is housebroken. The technical name for this practice is *coprophagy*.

Inoculations

If you have taken over your Shepherd before he is nine weeks old, he may not have had his Distemper and other inoculations. This you will have inquired about from the seller. We do not propose to give any hard and fast rules here concerning inoculations, as these vary with the new methods which are constantly being introduced.

It is a good plan to consult your veterinarian and take his advice. When the shots are given, check the puppy's temperature each day for the three days following, as some react and even suffer from "serum shock," although with modern vaccines this is comparatively rare. You will want the puppy inoculated primarily against Distemper, Hepatitis and Leptospirosis, these being the "killer" diseases in dogs. Your veterinarian will advise you if there are other shots which it is desirable he receive in your area. You must not on any account take your newly inoculated puppy out on the street or among other dogs during the period immediately following the shots. Nor should you, of course, take a puppy who has not been inoculated into public at all.

Worms

Your new baby will undoubtedly have been dosed for Roundworms before leaving his breeder, as this is usually done when the puppies are five or six weeks old. Inquire whether this was done and the product used. The dose should be repeated in 11 or 12 days, and the method is given under "Parasites" later in the book. We like to give a further dose at six months, to insure that the blood stream is quite clean. Professor Lambert, the famous Irish veterinarian, maintains that if young bitches are thoroughly dosed for Roundworm just before their first period of heat, they will be unlikely to pass on the worm infection to their puppies later in life. Since a bitch can come into season any time after her sixth month it is wise to attend to this important detail early.

When you take your puppy away from his home kennel, ask if you may maintain contact by telephone or letter, or even visit the breeder briefly once or twice during the first year for him to check up on growth, habits, and so on. An experienced eye can detect any faults or defects which can be remedied by medical attention or training, and it will reassure you to know that the breeder is behind you in your efforts to rear a first class German Shepherd Dog.

We have dwelt at length on the early puppyhood of your German Shepherd since this is a book primarily for those who are new to the breed. When you have mastered these simple rules and have learned how to care for your dog's health and hygiene, you can take the next step forward into training classes or the exhibition world with a healthy well-adjusted animal at your side.

Punishment and reward are the two keys to training your Shepherd. When he does well, praise and reward him; when he deliberately misbehaves, speak severely to him. A Shepherd will understand from your tone of voice and manner that you are displeased.

VI Early Training

If you keep your puppy indoors you will do well to remember that young dogs are no respecters of good furniture or treasured possessions. So until your puppy is trained, pack up your precious goods and chattels, roll up your beautiful rugs, and never leave him alone where he can get into mischief and do damage.

When he misbehaves speak to him firmly right from the start, coupling the reprimand with his name: " Kim, stop !" Kim, no," and so on. Do not be self-indulgent and spoil him because you fear he will not show as much affection if you are strict. A dog is " made" in the

PRUDENCE WALKER

How to loop a slip or choke chain.

first six months of his life. He has much to learn and you must begin early — not so much by what is known as obedience training, but in fashioning his behavior, checking his bad habits and generally guiding him in a pattern of civilized living.

The hand should only be used to caress a dog. Never slap a dog with the hand or you may make him hand shy, something that is pitiful in a pet and a major disqualification fault in a show dog. We use a loosely rolled up newspaper secured with a rubber band to give a tap on the rump or nose when a puppy misbehaves badly. The noise is more of a deterrent than the blow which is harmless, and after a few occasions it is usually sufficient merely to show him the roll and he will know that he has offended. Normally we give the young delinquent a short, sharp shake at the time of the voiced reprimand. Again this can do no harm, provided one keeps cool — even when he has chewed a heel off your new shoes!

The German Shepherd likes to please. You will find that a quiet, firm voice and gentle handling will bring good results in a surprisingly short time provided you are consistent. We like a house pet to start wearing a thin slip chain of suitable length, neither too long nor too short — one with about three or four inches more than the girth of his neck is about right. Put this chain on (see illustration) for a few minutes at a time and gradually increase the period until he is wearing it most of the day. A fine, light chain will not wear down his neck furnishings but a leather collar will.

When a visitor comes to the house, especially a mailman or delivery boy, slip your finger inside the chain and draw the puppy

A fine, light chain will not wear down his neck furnishings, but a leather collar might.

forward with you to the door, speaking encouragement as you move: "Good Boy! Come and say hello!" or "Good Kim, come to see who's here!" In this way your companion will come to understand that he is expected to greet callers, and keeping your hand on his chain insures that he will never jump up and annoy a well-dressed friend. Right from the start he will know that his place is beside you.

Teach him to "Shake Hands" by lifting his paw to the visitor's outstretched hand. If your friend is cooperative, ask him to reward the puppy with some small tidbit which you will have ready, or at least to praise him warmly: "Good Kim, good boy!"

To those who argue that they do not wish their pet to welcome callers I would answer that I have yet, after well over thirty years of experience, to own a German Shepherd who could not instantly recognize an unwanted caller. In fact, I have learned to reserve judgment of my new acquaintances who did not get the customary "Big Hello" from my dogs!

You must be very careful not to let your dog develop any bad habits during his early life, or you will have a "problem child" on your hands later on and get no pleasure from your bad mannered companion. So be firm now, using the same commands to control him time after time in a clear, decisive tone; your dog will soon learn that you mean what you say.

Staying Off Furniture

Among the troublesome habits a dog develops are jumping up, getting onto chairs or beds, stealing, and excessive barking.

If he climbs on your chairs to snooze, first ask yourself if his own bed is as good; perhaps it is in a draft, or has become too small, or is located in such a spot that he cannot watch you and the family. Remember that he is always "on duty," and wants at all times to be where he can keep his vigil. When you are satisfied on these points, try to anticipate his jump onto your bed or armchair. Jerk him off and put him firmly on his own bed, ordering him sternly, "Kim, Stay!" Follow the same procedure if you discover him sleeping on the furniture when you return home. Back to his own bed and hold him there for two or three minutes, commanding him to "Stay!"

While he's still a puppy — and, of course, that's when this disciplinary training should begin — utter a sharp "No!" and emphasize it with the crack of a rolled up newspaper. If a newspaper isn't close at hand at the critical moment, toss a book, magazine, or tin plate to land flat at his side. Don't hit him--startle him! If he doesn't see you tossing it, so much the better--he'll think it's a bolt from the blue!

Food Stealing

Stealing food is not so easy to cure. Some dogs are born thieves; the only remedy in their case is to keep all food out of reach. Some trainers fill some tasty tidbit with strong mustard and let the thief help himself from the table, and burn his mouth. As with all correction, prevention is better than cure; a dog which is never encouraged to come to the table or not allowed to receive handouts during his master's mealtimes is less likely to help himself. Chocolates and candies are not for him, anyway, so do not let him get excited by the sound of a candy box being opened. He can have his own store of doggy treats—some goodies or cubes of plain cheese, if you want to give him a tidbit when you are eating candy.

Barking

Excessive barking is not only annoying to you, it is also annoying to those who live nearby. Worse, you might come to ignore the dog's warnings, and end up by being surprised by an unwelcome visitor. Here again, do your best to prevent the barking habit from developing in early puppyhood. Never excite your puppy into boisterous games that make him rush around and bark, unless you also teach him to stop on command. If he does get overly excited, pick him up or put your arms around him and talk gently to him in a soothing voice. Put him back on his bed or in his kennel for a while, using the command, "Kim, Quiet!" If he barks when you leave him alone (which is normal as he will feel lonely deprived of company), pretend to go out and leave the door unfastened. Then when he starts to bark rush in and scold him, return him to his bed and soothe him down. Always leave him a bone or rubber toy to play with.

PRUDENCE WALKER

How to adjust a muzzle made of a strip of old cloth.

Details of the muzzle in place.

Dogs seem to imitate each other's behavior and, unfortunately, like children, they are more apt to acquire bad habits than good ones. The author is watching some of her dogs at play. Any tendency to misbehave is corrected at once before it develops into a bad habit.

For a difficult case of bad barking, try slipping a long folded slip of old linen over his muzzle (see page 93) and hold it there for a time while you shake your finger at him and firmly repeat, " Kim, Quiet!". You may have to resort to correction a number of times before he becomes reliable but your pleasure in a well behaved dog will more than compensate you for time spent on these early lessons.

If he is barking outdoors and won't stop on command, try dashing a pail of cold water on him.

Remember that the Shepherd is a dog bred to work under man's orders, gifted with great intelligence; he will delight in pleasing you, once you have learned to convey your commands clearly. He will make a spirited resistance at first, but that is as it should be; nobody gets any pleasure out of a " yes man" dog who has lost his independence. Once he shows signs of understanding, praise him quickly, repeat the command and praise him again. Time and patience will be well spent if you " make haste slowly."

Good Influences

We must now consider the importance of environmental influence on your puppy. Just as children follow a bad example quicker than a good one, so will your puppy. If you already have an older dog take great care that the young pup does not copy his less desirable habits. Similarly, if you have a neighbor whose dog rushes up and down the dividing fence barking and complaining, do not allow your puppy to emulate this bad habit. It is exhausting and wrong for a young puppy to get so excited. Ideally he should have a small enclosed pen in your yard where he can enjoy the fresh air in good weather without digging up your lawn or rose bushes. We go into details of his outdoor accomodation later in this book.

Do not allow highly strung or nervous members of your family to exercise the new puppy since, by flying into a panic over some small difficulty, they may ruin his character. If the puppy must be exercised by others than yourself, make certain they understand the importance of maintaining a calm attitude under all circumstances.

Check the dog at once for any fierce reactions, or for chasing after delivery men, or attempting to run after moving vehicles. Take hold of his slip chain and order him to sit, calm him down, then praise him. But the lesson of not doing these dangerous and annoying things is only learned in early days by a sharp reproof followed by praise when order has been restored.

Leash Training

So here you are with your puppy both housebroken and inoculated. The next step in his education is to accustom him to the leash. You have already had him wearing his light slip chain for some time each day, and he no longer feels strange or resents the restriction on his

During the early stages of leash training, be gentle; call and encourage him to walk alongside you while guiding him with the leash.

neck. While we are on this subject, it is right to warn you not to leave the dog alone at any time, or allow him to wander when out exercising, with the slip chain on his neck. Only this year, a friend lost a valuable dog who jumped over a wall and caught her chain on a nail — she died horribly by hanging.

If you want your dog to wear an identification tag when out on his walks, he must wear an extra-light leather collar in addition to his slip chain. The latter is used only for control. Take your puppy outside to a quiet place and sit him down at your left side. Fasten the lead to his chain, lift up his chin so that he is looking at you, and give him the command, " Kim, Heel!", stepping out and giving a gentle pull on the leash which is held in your right hand and controlled with your left.

The puppy is most likely to jerk away from you to the full length of his lead and behave like a fish on a line for a few minutes. However, you must coax him back to your left side, and calm him down with warm encouragement, " Good Kim, good dog! Sit!" When order is restored, repeat the whole procedure. You must exercise great patience at this early lesson. Treat it lightly and make your puppy think it is great fun; give him hearty praise, and a small tidbit such as a cube of cheese or of baked liver when the lesson is over. Don't be discouraged if you make very little progress in the first day or days. Try to keep him at it a total of ten minutes each day, and by the end of the week you will see results.

All your pleasure in taking your dog out will depend on his walking by your side and not pulling ahead, exhausting your strength and patience. So a couple of weeks spent over these short, daily lessons are a good investment for you both. When the puppy has stopped jerking ahead and bucking, you can continue the walk, gradually turning

SALLY ANNE THOMPSON

When teaching a puppy to " Come," the trainer must never lose patience or become irritated. Small tidbits and a coaxing manner are most effective. A light 20 foot check cord will keep him from wandering too far.

slightly left in a wide circle all the time. This will keep him close to you and he will get used to moving with his head near your leg. Then, when you stop, he will also stop as a matter of course, with only a slight check on the lead.

We do not advocate road exercise, or at any rate long walks, until the sixth month; but you can take your puppy about with you in your car and to public places so that he is accustomed to noises and people, and if he is properly leash-trained, he will be a safe and acceptable member of society.

Come When Called

The only other command which he *must* learn in his first six months is the recall to his name. Obedience to the recall is perhaps the first real test of the bond of understanding and respect between you and your dog. Never call the dog needlessly or he will grow bored. Call his name and give the command in a clear, cheerful tone, "Kim, Come!" Clap your hands or whistle to attract him, meanwhile standing perfectly still. When he comes, take hold of him, welcome him affectionately, try to "catch his eye" and make him look up to you. Give him praise and a small tidbit. If the lesson is given before meals the tidbit will be more effective. If you yell at your dog in an angry or disagreeable tone you will only frighten him, and even if you do succeed in attracting his attention he will return with ears pinned back and a dejected air which is no compliment to yourself. We have only to cast our mind back to our own childhood to remember which tone of voice gets the joyous answer!

Some trainers advocate teaching a puppy the recall by using a long — up to 20 feet — light check cord. With this fastened to his slip chain he is allowed to roam about. At the appropriate moment when his attention is elsewhere, his name is called and the check cord lightly jerked to attract his attention. Should he fail to respond to calls and the proferred tidbit, he can be gently reeled in. When he reaches you, he should be petted, praised and given his tidbit, just as though he had come on his own initiative.

The German Shepherd has an "anxious to please and obey" nature, and therefore he is as sensitive as he is responsive. So you must develop ties of affection coupled with firmness by keeping cool and repeating his lessons frequently, so that this precious relationship is established in the first half year.

The author and some of her dogs taking their morning exercise. Kennel dogs need human companionship, and if they are not to become morose and suspicious they should be handled and have human companionship at regular intervals.

VII   Outdoor Kennels

It is not likely that a beginner will want to go in for a lot of kenneling. But we would feel remiss not to mention a few points that may be helpful when you are ready to consider it—even if it's for a lone German Shepherd.

The location, if you have a choice, is to be considered first. Choose a well-drained area, and build the kennel at the highest point facing south or southwest if possible, or at least, in a spot sheltered from the prevailing winds. If an exercise enclosure is to surround the kennel, it is advantageous to have trees or bushes to provide a windbreak and some shade in summer, but never so much as to make the kennel dark or damp from water dripping after rains. If the ground surface is level without good drainage, construct a concrete base for the house first, about two or three feet larger each way than the frame of the kennel. This will keep the floor dry and prevent rats from burrowing underneath. It will also make the kennel easier to clean.

Cheap, wooden kennels are a false economy. A badly-housed dog will soon develop rheumatism and kidney chills, and all the nasty versions of cold and cough. Since these are expensive to treat and cure, a good, well-insulated doghouse can save its cost many times just by keeping the doctor away. Naturally, the choice of construction material will be influenced by the climate in which you live, so let local construction rules be your guide. For example, in one very warm country we saw kennel roofs thickly insulated against the strong sun, but they were raised about a foot from the walls so that air circulated freely and kept the atmosphere comfortable. It is best to paint the kennel a light color. It will be much cooler when the sun beats down.

In a temperate climate it is a good plan to buy a first-quality wooden shed of the type used for housing garden tools or bicycles. There are good ones made of strong weatherproofed cedar wood: one of these, measuring about six by nine feet and high enough for an average person to stand upright in, will kennel two dogs comfortably, or a bitch and her litter.

A shed measuring about six by nine feet, and high enough for an average person to stand upright in, will comfortably kennel two dogs, or a bitch and her litter.

PRUDENCE WALKER

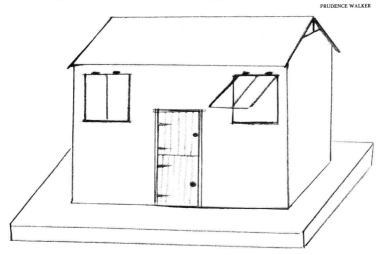

The shed should be lined with strong, closely fitted hardboard, and the space between the lining and the cedarwood, particularly the roof, well filled with insulating material. This will keep the dog cool in summer and warm in winter, and prevent many a chill when cold winds blow on the sleeping animal. The shed should be fitted with a door and a window. The window should open outwards from hinges at the top, so that it can be left open for ventilation on wet days without rain being blown inside.

For further ventilation in very hot weather we have a sliding door over an opening high up at the back of the kennel: this provides cross drafts of fresh air over the dog's head. It is also useful for drying out the kennel after it has been scrubbed.

We cover the inside of the door with a sheet of zinc, as we do the edges of any beds made of wood: a bored or mischievous dog will often chew his kennel, but few will attempt to make a meal of metal sheeting.

The floor comes in for some real beauty treatment. First, it is well rubbed with sandpaper, and any knot holes or cracks filled in with plastic wood filler. Second, it is given a thin coat of yacht (deck) varnish: third, a second coat when the first one is thoroughly dry. This insures a dry and sanitary kennel, even with small puppies, since the floor can be swept and washed frequently and will dry quickly because moisture cannot penetrate the varnish. A rub-over with sandpaper and a fresh coat of deck varnish may be necessary two or three times a year, more if many litters are reared.

The inside walls should be primed, undercoated, then finished with good quality enamel of the washable type often recommended for bathrooms and kitchens. Do not use an oil-based paint. A clear, bright color gives an impression of freshness, and wiping with a damp cloth

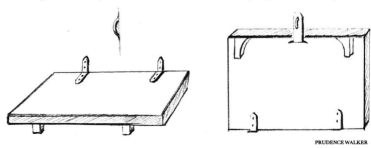

PRUDENCE WALKER

A sleeping bed fastened to a wall, let down ready for use.

Six beautiful Shepherds from the Duranburg Shepherd Kennel, owned by Simon and Myrtle Funderburg, of California. These dogs are bred not only for show, but also for disposition. Many are trained as obedience and guide dogs.

and light disinfectant is all that is required for maintenance.

The dog's bed can be one of several types according to taste and climate. The drop-down kind, hung from strong bracket hinges, with two legs which drop into position when it is lowered, is a practical solution when the dogs cannot be put outside in bad weather, as it can be raised against the wall leaving the floor space clear.

A board should be fitted across the front edge of the bed to hold the bedding in, and to keep the sleeper cozy, with the usual strip of zinc fastened along the rim to prevent chewing.

If preferred, a wooden bed on four short legs, with a ledge all round can be used; or one of the many commercial dog beds of metal and slung canvas.

101

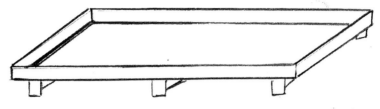

A sleeping platform, or a bed on four short legs with a ledge all around

Make sure that any window glass is securely fixed and protected with hardware cloth. If you have severe winters or long rainy seasons, cover the outside of the roof with thick roofing material, and see that a gutter carries the water well away from the walls.

Good kennels can be constructed inside barns or garages if these are already on the property, remembering always that any outside walls should be insulated in the manner described above. However, in these lofty buildings, which are ideal in summer or warm climates, it must be remembered that the dog loses a lot of body heat when sleeping, and will require more cozy quarters in winter. One has only to notice how a dog curls up and buries his nose in his tail on a cold day to appreciate that in his natural state he will dig himself a snug hole in a sheltered place, and there generate enough body heat to keep himself comfortably warm while asleep. Therefore, sleeping benches or beds should have some covering above them to keep in the body heat. A wooden canopy is ideal, or the dogs can be given sleeping boxes. These too will require zinc sheeting all round the edges to prevent chewing.

If winters are short, and one wishes to spare the expense of building permanent protection, a large tarpaulin (like those used on farms for covering hay) can be suspended above the sleeping quarters. This will give added comfort if the bedding is adequate. Wood shavings, or straw, with a clean burlap bag to curl up on placed on top, will keep the dog snug and warm.

In converting a building into a kennel it is essential that the right floors be laid, concrete being the most practical. A slight "fall" or slope toward a deep gutter or drain, which runs the length of the building is helpful for washing down. The outlet to this central drain should be large and adequate, and covered with a metal grid to avoid mishaps.

If the exercising run is of grass, it should be divided into two parts, so that one can be closed off and "rested" for a couple of weeks from time to time after having been sprinkled with lime or some similar agent. A run paved with fine gravel is perhaps the best provided the dogs are positively free from intestinal parasites. Any run which is constantly in use can become a source of infection, even if the droppings are disposed of daily (as they should be), so the layout should be planned accordingly. Where males are kept, a few posts with concrete around the base which can be hosed down daily will greatly help sanitation.

Some strong low wooden benches should be kept inside the run for the dogs to rest on when tired of romping; it is very dangerous, for puppies particularly, to lie about on damp grass or concrete — even in warm weather they can become chilled. If these benches are tilted up at night they will stay dry and last for years when given an occasional painting with creosote to preserve and disinfect them. A good makeshift bench can be constructed from an old door, with rough 4-inch timbers fixed across each end and the middle. Remove any metal fittings which might harm the inquisitive or bored animal.

PRUDENCE WALKER

Details of the properly constructed entrance to a kennel.

A trick we learned many years ago is to have a "dome" of concrete at the entrance to the run. This raises the area on either side of the gate so that puddles or mud do not collect where the dogs invariably spend much of their time, and where the grass disappears from the constant going to and from of two and four footed passers-by. The entrance gate will obviously have to be hung a little higher to clear the "dome." We like to have pebbles, small rocks and bricks near the entrance to exercise the dogs' feet and keep the nails short. Since all dogs naturally gravitate towards the gate, they cannot bypass this rough surfacing.

Now a word about heating. We like the infra-red lamps which are normally used by pig breeders. A lamp of this type, placed fairly high, will keep a large area cozy for German Shepherds who require little heat except during illness or when whelping. Great care should be taken to see that all control switches and exposed electrical connections are outside the kennel, or in any event, far above the reach of the most energetic dog; terrible accidents may result from electrocution or fire.

If several dogs are kept, an incinerator for burning soiled bedding and droppings will be required. A little kerosene carefully poured over the debris will help it to burn quickly. All kennels and runs require daily cleaning and mild disinfecting since dogs dislike strong carbolic smells just as much as we do.

Beds should be scrubbed at least once a week and floors and concrete areas hosed down daily. All soiled bedding should be removed immediately and replaced with clean, and a keen eye kept open for any insect pests. The Vapona bar, described in Chapter XVI, will be of great help here.

If you are a one dog owner who prefers to keep his dog outside, build the solitary kennel near the house to obviate the dog's sense of loneliness which is often detrimental to temperament. Place his exercising run where you can see each other when going out and coming in, so that you can take a few moments to reassure him and pat his head. It will ease his isolation, even if it is only temporary.

We have a glassed-in porch attached to our house where three or four dogs sleep to protect us since we live in a lonely location. Thus they are a part of the main establishment without any inconvenience to us, and they are warmly housed and can be visited frequently. The goodnight ritual takes a long time with each dog rolling over and begging for one more caress!

Remember, when you plan your dog's diet, that feeding time is the most important time of his day.

VIII Feeding the German Shepherd

Remember when you plan your dog's diet that feeding time is the most important time of his day. If he is a normal healthy dog, his mealtimes will be a much anticipated joy. He cannot tell you his likes and dislikes, nor does he take into account what is good for him. It is up to you to use your knowledge to give him the right food, in the right amount and at the right time of day.

Some owners prefer to plan their dog's diets and prepare the food themselves; others rely on packaged dog foods. First let us consider some general feeding procedures and then examine both methods.

Quality

To begin with, the food must be of good quality. Anything less will not keep the dog healthy and in fine coat. It is false economy to feed scraps and offal as substitutes for good nutritious dog food. Certainly, as a change, organ meat like liver, heart, kidney and tripe may be given and it will be much appreciated, but as a regular diet these foods do not provide the needed body building nutriments.

The preparation of meat, if you use fresh meat in the diet, is especially important, for it should not be overcooked. Often one hears of the breeder who keeps a stockpot going for the dog, and in it the meat is boiled until most of the essential nutriments have been destroyed by heat. This is neither good for the German Shepherd who is to be shown, the busy stud dog or the brood bitch, nor does it really satisfy the companion dog who admittedly does not lead their energetic lives.

Temperature

Food and drink should always be served at the right temperature, neither too cold nor too hot. Food taken out of the refrigerator and fed at once may cause Gastritis or some other digestive trouble. On the other hand, a meal that is too hot will upset the dog and put him off his feed. Dogs will not eat food as hot as a human palate can tolerate. The ideal temperature is slightly tepid. Drinks for puppies should be given at an approximate temperature of 70.°

Cleanliness

This is another important point. Bowls should be kept scrupulously clean, and washed thoroughly after each meal. Putting the food into the dish still on the floor from the last meal, and sometimes even on top of the food that is left, is a dreadful habit. It should not be the least surprising if the dog has no appetite, or suffers from digestive upsets.

Then again, the German Shepherd must be comfortable in his eating place. He should not be expected to eat in a chilling wind, or in burning sun, or in the rain. His dining place should be cool, dry and clean. He should have ample opportunity to relieve himself before eating, but he should not be shut out for so long a period before mealtime that he feels neglected and upset before he starts to eat.

Time and Place

A regular timetable should be adhered to. Meals are of great importance to all dogs. They have a biologically built-in clock which tells them when dinner ought to be ready. Therefore, if his meal is late your dog is going to fret, and unless there is some good reason for the delay, do not cause him anxiety.

German Shepherds with varying dispositions need different handling when it comes to feeding. A shy and nervous dog will often do more justice to his meal if he is fed alone. The fear of a dog with a more dominant personality, eating in the same place, may completely upset him. On the other hand, a "choosey" and uninterested feeder may feed much better if another dog, or even a cat, is in the same room, because natural protection of his property will spur him on.

Balance and Variety

There is no doubt that if you are to feed your dog to his full physical and mental growth, and compound his diet yourself, a great deal of time, trouble, forethought, patience and even psychology must be employed. When planning the German Shepherd's diet, two points must be considered: food must be of the highest quality, and the diet must be balanced.

Hard-working Shepherds like this one can burn up excess calories. However, family pets, which lead a more sedentary life, should have their diets carefully watched and reduced at the first sign of overweight.

PURINA PET CARE CENTER

Feeding foodstuffs of high quality is in itself an economy, for good health will result, obviating the expense of extra tonics and appetizers and minimizing veterinary bills. A balanced diet must contain the correct proportions of proteins, carbohydrates and fats. Proteins are supplied by meat, fish, eggs, and cheese, and carbohydrates by cereals, biscuits, bread, and potatoes. The fat proportion is found in a certain amount of fatty meat, fish oils, and the butter content of milk or the fat in margarine. Since milk also contains protein and minerals, it often has a place in many diets.

Variety in the diet keeps the German Shepherd's appetite normal and keen, but it is really not essential as those who feed the same prepared food day after day can attest.

How Much Food?

If you feed fresh meat, to gauge the amount of food required, feed half an ounce of good quality lean meat to every pound of body weight. Thus the young dog weighing 14 to 16 pounds will need seven to eight ounces of meat daily. But to this *must* be added dog meal or other supplements.

If a dog who is normally a good feeder refuses his food, or appears to have little enthusiasm for it, his temperature should be taken immediately, as this may well be the first symptom of some disease or infection. If you are perceptive enough to notice this sign right at the beginning, you may prevent more serious trouble.

Main Meal

This can be fed at any time convenient after noon. In hot weather it is best given in the early evening: two or three handfuls of commercial kibble, one tablespoonful of raw, finely grated carrot, one tablespoonful chopped watercress and/or parsley, 1½ to 2½ pounds of fresh meat, part of which can be fish, or cottage cheese. A small cupful of boiling broth can be used to mix the meat and kibble, and one teaspoonful each of pure olive oil and halibut liver oil may be added just before feeding. The oil will stick to the sides of the bowl and be wasted if it is added during the mixing.

Bedtime — Cupful of half milk and half water, large dog biscuit to chew and help keep the teeth clean, a cube of well boiled liver or a large beef bone which can also serve as his " tooth brush."

The German Shepherd is not as a rule a greedy feeder, although there are some notable exceptions. This female has been fed too much and exercised too little. Her meals must be cut down and her exercise time increased, if she is not to fall victim to the maladies attendant upon obesity.

Variations — Give fish instead of meat occasionally, and add a couple of egg yolks (discard the white if fed raw). Organ meat can also make up half the meat ration on occasion. Do not cut the meat up too small. Large chunks weighing two or three ounces are about right and give exercise to jaws and teeth, provoking saliva and assisting the digestion. Ground meat, strangely, does not digest as easily as meat in chunks.

Appetite

A well exercised dog in good health will eat heartily although the amount he might eat will vary a little, as it does with humans, due to the rate of metabolism and variables like size, age and temperament. A lively energetic dog will always consume more than one with a quiet, placid disposition, although both may be in perfect health. Any healthy dog will eat about one third more than he needs for daily living, so always underfeed a little.

The German Shepherd is not as a rule a greedy feeder, although there are some notable exceptions — usually the ones that put on weight easily — and it is always a hard task to reduce their food intake. A dog's digestive processes take about nine hours (that is for the adult). It can easily be calculated what harm feeding dainties does during this interval, just as it is harmful to give a child candy between meals. The fact that the dog *will* eat does not mean that he *should* eat and you must be severe with your family and friends if they offer him tasty morsels at table. In my estimation, sugar, particularly, is a great enemy of the dog and you must explain that too much indulgence in sweets can shorten your pet's life.

If the dog's appetite is poor or erratic, check for worms, (Tape or Round) and note if the dog is constipated or if the bowel movement is irregular. Normally, stools are passed twice daily in an active animal and once in an older or less energetic one. A puppy may have five or six.

Some kennels practice the habit of a weekly fast day, and this is highly recommended by the natural health practitioners. However, it is not so easy with a house pet, although once the routine is established the dog seems to accept the day of abstinence without objection. The plan is to leave him for one day on water only, or if you feel it is less harsh, half milk and half water with a small quantity of honey or Karo, particularly in winter when the fasting dog may feel chilled if he is deprived of all nourishment. Milk, of course, is food, Karo is glucose — a sugar — so if you give very much the dog is really not fasting.

I like to feed a small meal of meat on the morning following the fast and the usual meal minus this portion of meat at the customary feeding time. Fasting is, of course, only practiced with adults, although a half day's fast is often beneficial to puppies at teething time when the digestion is disturbed. Purging is recommended at the conclusion of a long fast. For large puppies give a dessert spoonful of milk of magnesia and for adults a large tablespoonful or the same quantity of mineral oil.

At about one year of age, a German Shepherd's frame is fully developed. He will continue to fill out for some time and will still require a growing phase. One meal a day, plus possibly a light supplemental feeding, should be sufficient.

If your dog does not eat heartily following this routine, it might be wise to take him to your veterinarian for a check up. The appetite really depends on a properly established rhythm and this should follow the one which nature herself planned for the dog in his wild state, when he would go forth to run and hunt, and having killed his prey would eat, then retire to sleep.

A wolf will eat a 20 pound meal and sleep two days, but sometimes he eats lemmings and other small rodents which do not glut him and he will continue hunting except for short rest intervals. Exercise should precede food, and sleep follow it. A dog will sometimes play with a companion, chew his bone or tease a toy after his meal, but sleep soon overcomes him as digestion gets under way and he should not be disturbed. His natural hours for rest and elimination are, approximately, from midnight to midday. So we like to feed the main meal between five and six p.m. Then the dog rests quietly during the evening, has his last exercise before midnight and is less drowsy during the early hours of the morning when he should be on duty as your watchdog. Again, with his rhythm working smoothly, he will be ready to exercise and eliminate at the first opportunity next morning. This program requires regular hours for feeding and exercising, the reward being a healthy pet who will live a long and happy life.

Commercial Foods

Nowadays, a tremendous amount of research goes into the production of dog foods. Tests for palatability, for growth of coat, for steady maintenance of condition — all with their supporting clinical studies — are carried out by many of the leading dog food manufacturers. Also vitamins and minerals and their corresponding values are exhaustively explored in laboratory tests, and then added to enrich many foodstuffs. So there is no reason why the modern dog should nog have in his diet every possible ingredient to enhance the condition of his body and coat, and also nourish his nervous system to aid in breeding puppies whose temperaments are steady and whose dispositions are pleasant.

An American authority on dog nutrition has stated that there are as many different diets for dogs as there are dogs. After all of the millions of dollars which have been spent on dog foods to make them complete in every nutritional respect, there are still those who ignore all of this research and insist on concocting their own mixtures. Probably no diet which the average dog owner can produce will be more nutritious, and by no means more complete or growth promoting, than the better grades of prepared foods for sale in almost all markets. Some are in cans (the more expensive kinds), some are ready to feed with the addition of water. Some are dried in the form of meal or pellets.

For economy the last two are the best. You are not paying for water. Most of the brands are deficient however in fat and so fat should be added — 10 to 15 % of the ration. Any edible fat will do, whether it be margarine made from vegetable oils, ground trimmings from the butcher's fat barrel or what have you — frying pan fat, fat removed from the top of a soup kettle; dogs love and digest it all.

We have no quarrel with those who want to spend time and money buying fresh meat, feeding eggs, milk and human foods to their dogs. But we do know that for kennel dogs, such a procedure is a great waste of time and money, and even a house pet will thrive on commercial foods.

It may be as difficult for dog owners, steeped in the old tradition of feeding so prevalent a generation ago, to change and adopt scientifically demonstrated facts about feeding, as it is for some persons to change their religions. "Time makes ancient good uncouth."

We know now that dogs do not need fresh muscle meat for they can live equally well on many other things such as fish or whale (which, of course, is mammalian). They can also live on animal proteins which have been dried. Dogs can not digest egg white; the raw yolk *is* digestible but it costs almost as much to feed one egg as it costs for an entire day's commercial ration. Dogs can digest starch if it is baked, and sweets also, and lots of other items. Some even relish various kinds of fruit.

To make feeding your pet German Shepherd or kennel of them as easy and economical as any method we can conceive, use high grade dry dog meal or kibble and add extra fat. This is good for every dog from weaning through old age.

Of course, if your dog is a home companion, and you can't resist his pleading eyes you can also treat him to a hard dog biscuit to help keep his teeth clean and his breath sweet. This is highly recommended provided you do not feed him so many as to make him overweight or spoil his appetite for his regular meal.

Nutrient Requirements

A great deal of work on dog nutrition is being done by governmental agencies. This work is not only investigatory but is also necessary because the government sets standards for pet food manufacturers. A summary of some of the findings of the Subcommittee on Canine Nutrition of the National Academy of Sciences condensed into chart form are given here.

Table I will be of interest to those who would like to prepare their own mix, and for those who are curious as to just what goes into a commercial dog food. It is a breakdown of two different meal-type rations.

Table I

Meal Type Rations for Dogs[1]
(Dry matter 91%)

Ingredient	Ration 1 %	Ration 2 %
Meat and bone meal, 55% protein	8.00	15.00
Fish meal, 60% protein	5.00	3.00
Soybean oil meal	12.00	— .
Soybean grits	— .	19.00
Wheat germ oil meal	8.00	5.00
Skim milk, dried	4.00	2.50
Cereal grains	51.23	— .
Corn flakes	— .	26.75
Wheat bran	4.00	— .
Wheat flakes	— .	26.70
Fat, edible	2.00	— .
Bone meal, steamed	2.00	— .
Brewers yeast, dried	2.00	0.50
Fermentation solubles, dried	1.00	— .
Salt, iodized	0.50	0.25
Vitamin A and D feeding oil (2,250 IU of A, 400 IU of D per gm)	0.25	0,50
Riboflavin supplement[2]	— .	0.80
Iron oxide	0.02	— .

[1] While these rations have been used satisfactorily with some dogs, there is no assurance that all dogs will accept them readily.
[2] BY-500.

Table II lists a dog's requirements in terms of food components per pound of body weight. It is interesting to note that growing puppies (last column) require two or more times as much of each of these nutrients as do adult dogs.

Table II

Nutrient Requirements of Dogs[1]
(Amounts per pounds of body weight per day)

	Weight of dog in pounds	Adult maintenance	Growing puppies
Energy (kcal)[2]	5	50	100
	10	42	84
	15	35	70
	30	32	64
	50 and over	31	62
Protein-minimum (gm)		2.0	4.0
Carbohydrate-maximum (gm)[3]		4.6	7.2
Fat (gm)		0.6	1.2
Minerals:			
Calcium (mg)		120	240
Phosphorus (mg)		100	200
Iron (mg)		0.600	0.600
Copper (mg)		0.075	0.075
Cobalt (mg)		0.025	0.025
Sodium Chloride (mg)		170	240
Potassium (mg)		100	200
Magnesium (mg)		5	10
Manganese (mg)		0.050	0.100
Zinc (mg)		0.050	0.100
Iodine (mg)		0.015	0.030
Vitamins:			
Vitamin A (IU)[3]		45	90
Vitamin D (IU)[3]		3	9
Vitamin E (mg)		—	1
Vitamin B12 (mg)		0.0003	0.0006
Folic acid (mg)		0.002	0.004
Riboflavin (mg)		0.020	0.040
Pyridoxine (mg)		0.010	0.020
Pantothenic acid (mg)		0.023	0.045
Niacin (mg)		0.110	0.180
Choline (mg)		15	30

While the amount of food required by a dog varies, depending on such things as the dog's own metabolism, activity, environment, and so on, as we have previously noted the greatest difference will be found between the requirements of a growing dog and an adult. Table III gives the estimated daily food intake required by dogs of various sizes, broken down into *Requirements for Maintenance* — this covers the average non-working dog under normal conditions — and *Requirements for Growth* — these are the amounts of food required by a growing dog. While some adjustments in these amounts may be required for your own pet, they do serve as guidelines when estimating how much to feed your dog. An old dog will probably require less food than indicated here, while a pregnant or nursing bitch will require more.

Table II footnotes

[1] *Symbols-gm — gram; mg — milligram; IU — International Unit.*

[2] *Values listed are for gross or calculated energy. Biologically available energy is ordinarily 75-85 per cent of the calculated.*

[1] *The values shown are based upon dry and canned foods containing 91 and 28 per cent dry matter. Moisture has been included to indicate general level of composition rather than as a requirement. There is no evidence that carbohydrate as such is required, but since it occurs as a part of many dog-food ingredients, a maximum value has been suggested.*

[2] *The 0.6 and 0.18 mg quanity of crystalline vitamin A is equal to 2000 and 600 IU, respectively. One mg vitamin A alcohol — 3,333 IU of vitamin A. One mg beta carotene — 1,667 IU of vitamin A activity. For dogs carotene is approximately one-half as valuable as vitamin A alcohol.*

[3] *These amounts of pure vitamin D correspond to 120 and 40 IU per pound of feed.*

Table III

Estimated Daily Food Intakes Required by Dogs of Various Sizes

| | Requirements for growth | | | |
| | Dry type foods[1] | | Canned dog food[2] | |
Weight of dog	Per lb body wt	Per dog	Per lb body wt	Per dog
lbs	lbs	lbs	lbs	lbs
5	0.040	0.20	0.120	0.60
10	0.033	0.33	0.101	1.01
15	0.028	0.42	0.085	1.27
20	0.027	0.54	0.081	1.60
30	0.025	0.75	0.077	2.30
50	0.025	1.25	0.075	3.74
70	0.025	1.75	0.075	5.23
110	0.024	2.64	0.074	8.22
	Requirements for maintenance			
	Dry type foods[1]		Canned dog food[2]	
Weight of dog	Per lb body wt	Per dog	Per lb body wt	Per dog
lbs	lbs	lbs	lbs	lbs
5	0.080	0.40	0.240	1.20
10	0.066	0.66	0.202	2.02
15	0.056	0.84	0.190	2.54
20	0.054	1.08	0.160	3.20
30	0.050	1.50	0.154	4.60
50	0.050	2.60	0.150	7.48
70	0.050	3.50	0.150	10.46
110	0.048	5.28	—	—

[1] *Dry foods contain 6-12 per cent moisture. Calculations of the amounts of dry food required have been based on energy supplied by food containing 91 per cent dry matter, 76 per cent protein plus carbohydrate, 5 per cent fat and 10 per cent ash, fiber and other inert material. This supplies a calculated 1583 kcal per pound, of which it is estimated that 80 per cent or 1266 kcal are digestible.*

[2] *Calculated on the basis of 28 per cent dry matter and the same nutrient ratios as in 1, with the total and available energy calculated as 490 and 415 (85 per cent of the total) kcal per pound.*

"We groom our dogs from puppyhood onwards on a bench or on a big old wooden table which we keep in the yard. This makes it less tiring on our backs and more comfortable to go over the dog for his daily checkup."

IX   Grooming

We groom our dogs from puppyhood onwards on a bench or on a big old wooden table which we keep in the yard. This makes it less tiring on our backs, and more comfortable to go over the dog for his daily check up. This way he becomes accustomed to being "vetted" on a table and will take it as a matter of course. When small, the puppy will have to be lifted onto the bench, but at five to six months he should be able to spring up by himself when invited.

When you have settled him on the bench, reassure him with your voice as you pass your hand under his belly to make him stretch out

118

into a show stance; use the command, "Kim, stand!" Position him with his front feet under his shoulders, not stuck out forwards, as this will spoil his balance and give him a wooden appearance. Then command him to sit, and tilting his head upwards with one hand, ease his lips upwards to show his dentition. First display the bite — that is, the front teeth where they meet in the desired "scissor bite." Then gentley lift the lips, first on one side and then on the other, to expose the premolars and aftermolars. If this is done gently the first time — with the reward of a small piece of cooked liver or a cube of cheese — the puppy will not resent these routine examinations. You will be over a big hurdle when it comes to exhibition training.

Next examine the ears. They should not be red or spotty. If they appear tender, look down into the base for evidence of canker; this manifests itself as a red-brown, thick discharge which gives off an acid, moldy odor. You can recheck this by wrapping a finger in a cleansing tissue and gently feeling inside the ear. Canker is difficult to cure, especially if it is not diagnosed in the early stages. (We deal with its treatment under "Parasites".) In any case, the ears should be cleaned weekly, either by wrapping a tissue round the finger and carefully loosening all dirt, or by wiping the inside gently with a cotton tipped swab moistened with sweet almond oil. Never pour any liquid into the dog's ear without your veterinarian's advice; it could cause pain and damage.

The teeth do not usually require cleaning during the first year or 18 months. However, if there are any stains on the enamel, dip a clean piece of old linen (an old handkerchief will do) into hydrogen peroxide and then into powdered pumice and rub the offending stain gently, afterwards rinsing well with clean warm water.

If his nose is dry or cracked, rub in a little white Vaseline gently. This is useful in very cold weather too, when noses have been rooting in the snow.

If the eyes are running, or there is any mucus in the inner corner, the dog may have gotten seeds in his eye. If he is exercised on the beach, his eyes may even be sore from the fine sea sand blowing into them. Another cause of minor eye injury is hay or straw, sometimes used for bedding. Seeds are present here, while straw can do damage with its sharp ends. Bathe with plenty of warm water and boric acid or use a human eye drop like "Murine," and squeeze a small amount of veterinary antibiotic ointment into each corner.

Now take a look at his feet to see if he has any thorns or cuts

Outdoor dogs should be examined regularly and carefully. Check the coat for burrs or parasites, the eyes for foreign matter, the pads for cuts or thorns, and the ears for any material that may have become lodged there.

between the toes, or cut pads and torn nails. All of these are painful and capable of causing lameness if neglected, yet easily soothed by bathing with a disinfectant solution and smearing with a recommended salve when dry. There are many of these canine ointments on the market, most of which give good results.

The tail should be lifted to inspect the anus and surrounding fur for any segments of tapeworm. Any prolonged soreness here calls for veterinary examination if it does not yield quickly to ointment. Bitches, of course, should be watched for any swelling of the vulva in order to be ready with security plans when her season commences. This can be ascertained by pressing her vulva gently with a folded Kleenex to see if there is any stain.

For grooming the coat we like to comb it thoroughly with a wide toothed metal comb, as large as can be comfortably held (too fine or close combs break the coat) and inspect the skin meanwhile by turning the fur back with the comb.

Next we use a good, stiff whalebone dandy brush, of the type used for ponies. Brush the coat really hard, first with a rotary action to cleanse and stimulate, then with short, hard sweeps of the brush to smooth the coat and make it gleam. Don't forget the legs and tail; but use a softer brush on the belly and flanks.

The grooming may be finished with one of the several kinds of gloves expressly made for this purpose or with a large, clean chamois. Bare patches on the elbows can be kept under control — and finally healed if taken in time — by the simple homemade remedy of equal quantities of white Vaseline and coconut oil melted together. Apply to the elbows and massage well into the skin, but take care that greedy dogs don't eat the salve, or they will be very sick.

Nail Care

If the dog does not get regular exercise on pavements his nails may easily grow too long, an ugly fault in a working breed like ours. Nails must be clipped with care. Use nail clippers especially designed for

It is wise to clip a very small bit of the nail at a time, examining the cut surface each time before proceeding.

dogs. Unless your German Shepherd is unusually cooperative you may need help—someone to clip, someone to hold. The foot must be kept steady or you may cut into the quick (the blood vessel feeding the nail), making him footsore for a long time. If you are a novice, it is wise to clip a very small amount at a time, examining the cut surface each time before proceeding. As you approach the quick, the texture of the nail will change from hard horn to spongy pulp and you will then know that you have cut far enough.

Grooming Kit

A wooden tray with compartments can easily be made by a do-it-yourself enthusiast, (see illustration) and it will help to make your grooming session more pleasant. Here is a list of items that will be helpful:

Brushes and steel comb
Chamois skin and grooming
    glove
Facial Tissue
Flea powder
Mild desinfectant for cuts, etc.
Plastic bag to hold hair-combings

Cotton
Elbow salve
Eye lotion and ointment
Nail clippers
Forceps to remove thorns or
    ticks

We suggest plastic containers since most tasks must be carried out with one hand, the other being needed to hold the dog. Avoid any kind of glass container as a struggling dog can knock it over and break it.

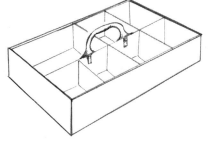

A wooden tray with compartments can easily be made by a do-it-yourself enthusiast, and it will help to make your grooming session more pleasant.

"It is considered a mistake to bathe the dog too often. It is amazing, though, after all the precautions we take to avoid chilling our dogs while bathing them, to find them leaping merrily into pools and ponds and other bodies of water, swimming gaily and happily about, without suffering any ill effects whatsoever."

Bathing

It is a mistake to bathe a dog too often. Too frequent bathing removes protective oils from the coat causing it to soil more quickly. Much depends on the conditions under which the dog is kept. German Shepherds kept mainly indoors may need more frequent bathing to do away with body odor. The bath may be given indoors or out, according to the weather. Any possible chance of chilling should be avoided. A warm sunny day should be chosen. Dampness indoors or out should cause a postponement to another day. The bathtub or a washtub is probably the most practical place to bathe a dog the size of the German Shepherd. Until he's full grown the kitchen sink may do. Place a mat or a rough towel on the bottom to keep him from slipping.

Equipment

First gather together everything that may be required. Once the bath has begun it is almost impossible to leave the dog to get some forgotten item. There are many excellent dog shampoos on the market; choose one recommended for the German Shepherd. Have at least two large warm towels and a chamois skin ready for drying. (The chamois should be kept solely for this purpose and not for cleaning the car or windows). Have a jar of Vaseline to smear around the rims of the eyes to prevent soap from getting in. A washcloth is useful for washing the face, and cotton wads should be used for plugging the ears to keep water out of them. A rubber shower spray is useful but not an absolute necessity; a sprinkling can will do very well. There should also be some source of quick warmth for drying: a heater, hot radiator, or an electric hairdrier. A waterproof apron for yourself is also a " must." In summer, a bathing suit will be practical.

The Bath

Put a few inches of warm water in the tub—about 100^0 F. will be about the right temperature. Stand the dog in the tub, but not before all mats and tangles have been combed out of his coat and his eyes and ears have been protected. Talk to him reassuringly as you go along. Splash water over him with your hands or a cup, but keep his head dry. Now apply the soap or shampoo. Start from the tail and work forward. Leave the head until last. Dogs object less vigorously to their bodies being bathed; it is when you reach the head that they become restless. Never use shampoo or soapy water on the head; just wipe it off with a damp cloth. Be extremely careful not to get water inside the ears.

Soap and rinse at least twice; for "squeaky" cleanness, a third round is not too much. Use the shower spray for rinsing, or the sprinkling can or large jugs of water. To make sure that all soap is removed, some groomers give a final rinse with vinegar and water.

Before removing the dog from the tub, check his hindquarters under the tail for cleanliness and, if the anal glands need squeezing, do it now. (See page 206).

After the final rinsing, throw a big towel around the dog before you let him out of the tub. Otherwise you will be deluged in the shower that is sure to follow when he shakes himself. Rub him dry as much as

German Shepherds are an active breed, and they need plenty of freedom to maintain the well-muscled appearance typical of a working dog.

possible and place him in a warm room with an added source of heat.

Additional towels may be needed; it is very important to get him dry just as quickly as possible. The chamois wrung out in very hot water and wiped over the dog will also help. Do not let him become chilled. Dogs are much more susceptible to chilling than are humans. If at all possible, use an electric hair drier.

Only if it is a hot summer's day should he be taken outdoors, and then be careful that he does not romp away and roll over and over the grass or in something obnoxious.

Do not forget to remove the cotton from the ears and to wipe the Vaseline from the eyes.

Now, as the coat dries, you can groom him as we described earlier.

Exercise

German Shepherds are an active breed, needing plenty of freedom to maintain the well-muscled appearance typical of a working dog. Road exercise is needed too, to maintain the short, tightly knit feet required by the standard.

In Europe one frequently sees a German Shepherd Dog being exercised by his owner slowly pedaling a bicycle along one of the lonely country roads. If one can find a track or road quiet enough, this is an easy way to exercise the dog. We are not entirely happy when a show dog is exercised in this manner. We feel that the stride is lengthened and the pace increased to a speed that is almost impossible for the human handler to keep up with in the ring.

If there are steps or cliffs to which you have access for exercising, it is excellent for shoulder development and for strengthening the feet and pasterns. Encourage your dog (but not before the age of six months) to climb them and retrieve some object that you have tossed. If you can only walk your dog on the leash for routine exercise, try to find some place, however small, where you can play with him off the leash: quoit retrieving, hide and seek, or going over a jump are some of the ways he can use his muscles.

You should not, however, teach him any rough games which involve you, nor should you let your children do it. Arm grabbing, seizing coat tails, and so on are perhaps amusing in a small puppy but in an adult they are dangerous. It is always wrong to allow a dog to take liberties with your person. He must reserve his teeth for intruders, and never nibble your hand or arm, even in fun.

To teach a dog to "Sit," hold him up by his collar with your right hand and press down on his hindquarters with your left, while repeating the command.

X   Obedience Training

Apart from housebreaking which has to be taught as soon as a puppy starts to live indoors — say at nine or ten weeks of age — and small lessons in civilized living such as a reprimand when he climbs onto forbidden furniture, no attempt at serious training should be made before he is three or four months of age, and then it should be kept to simple companion dog training. All advanced instruction should wait until his first birthday.

To train a dog you must first gain his affection and confidence. In other words, you will both learn during the first lessons. He will learn that you are his master and that when he is hungry his food comes from your hands. He will also learn that you play with him, scratch his ears, tickle his chest, offer other pleasant sensations, and that the day begins when you take him outside and ends when you put him to bed with bone or biscuit and a goodnight fuss. You will learn about his early reactions — if he is upset by certain noises or odors, if he likes or dislikes children or women (or men), and you will discover any other indications that can guide you in his future training.

While it is well known that a dog's eyesight is not nearly as keen as his sense of smell or hearing, it is not so widely known that German Shepherds have only moderate sight. Once when I was a house guest at Giralda, my hostess, Mrs. Geraldine Rockefeller Dodge — who will certainly go down in history as one of the best informed and most experienced breeders in the world — told me that they had once made tests on dogs' vision among the many breeds kept there — Cocker Spaniels, Golden Retrievers, Bloodhounds, Rottweilers and German Shepherds. They concluded that the Rottweilers had the keenest sight and that German Shepherds had the least keen! This may account for our breed's suspicion of strangers and strange objects and its nervous reactions to sudden and unaccustomed noises. Their ears respond but their eyes do not, leaving the dogs confused.

It is curious how the early lessons of what we call "civilizing" can count for so much in a dog's adult life. Long ago we had a much loved dog who was a fine character, full of reasoning and initiative and brave enough to tackle wild animals when he went to Canada with us; but he was terrified of laundry flapping on the line or cloths or dusters being shaken near him, and since we valued him highly we had to consider what to do to prevent this from developing in other German Shepherds. We decided that the early formative weeks were the time to instill tolerance or indifference to flapping clothes, and strung clothesline across the puppies' run. Now they grow up familiar with the flutterings and sounds of clothes blown by the wind. We have even suffered the loss of some laundry that was blown loose and seized as playthings by the irreverent babies. And we have found that any new object, if it is introduced to the nose first, will afterwards be accepted. By recognizing the dog's limitations of sight, the trainer's hand is strengthened. He can adjust his methods of teaching.

You will have taught your puppy to walk on leash as suggested in an earlier chapter. Make sure as he grows that you replace the slip chain collar with a longer one. When he is fully grown it should measure at least 25 inches. Always allow plenty of slack in the chain so that you can jerk it up to check the puppy; it will not spoil the neck ruff then as it slackens off as soon as you (or the puppy) cease pulling. The noise of the chain being pulled through the ring is associated in the dog's mind with the order, "Kim, heel", and he will learn to expect control from both voice and hand in conjunction with this sound. Soon he will realize that unless he eases up and trots close to your side he will experience the sharp jerk and crisp command. This slip chain, your voice and hands are all that you need for this early training, apart from a good quality leather leash and the ever-necessary inexhaustible supply of patience.

Fetch

Here are a few simple games that can be played indoors which will provide the basis for mutual exercise when the weather is too bad for long walks. Puppies like to carry things in their mouths—we have all lost shoes, books, gloves, and so forth, because of their passion for collecting articles, not always to chew them, but just for the joy of possession. So if we are going to teach our dog to retrieve later on, we will do well to make use of this habit. A medium sized chamois skin is a good article to start with. It is soft to the tender mouth and light to carry, and it can be washed out when it grows soiled from use. Shake the skin to get him interested and then throw it a short distance, using whatever command we intend to keep for his training, preceded as always by his name: " Kim, fetch" or " Kim, carry" in a coaxing tone. He may bound after the object or merely stare at it and at you in

" Fetch!" is a useful command, and once he has learned its meaning he can be taught to retrieve all sorts of articles. Here he is learning to retrieve a dumbbell. It is dropped so close to his nose that he can reach it just by lowering his head. Give the command and slip the dumbbell into his mouth.

SALLY ANNE THOMPSON

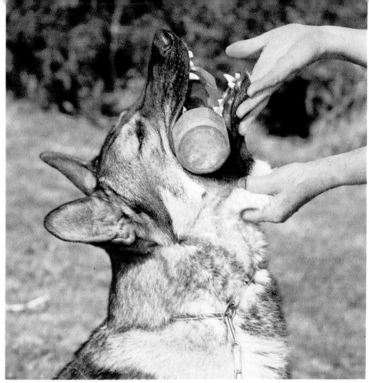

Once the object is retrieved, he must learn to hold it until commanded, "Drop!" Hold his head up and stroke his chin, not only to prevent his dropping the object, but also as a reward. Keep repeating the command, "Hold!" After a few minutes, allow him to drop his head and release the object as you say, "Drop!"

bewilderment; if this happens, lead him forward to the skin and shake it until he seizes it. Then go back again with the puppy beside you, throw the skin with the command when he should dash forward to get it. You may have to do this several times until the idea sinks in and he finds it fun.

When he does eventually pick up the skin be prompt with a lot of praise: "Clever dog, Kim" in a delighted voice so that he feels enthusiasm, even if you *are* weary. Do not force the skin into the puppy's mouth. If he is hurt during these first exercises it may make him diffident forever about retrieving or carrying. It is better to tease him a bit by shaking it to gain his interest.

When he has fetched or picked up the skin a few times you can continue on to his next lesson by walking away and patting your left leg to entice him to follow; then stop and bend over to gently open the puppy's mouth with your left hand and extract the skin with your right. You may have to corner him at first so that he cannot get away and you must be quietly firm with your command, " Kim, *Drop!*" as you take the skin. Praise him afterwards; pat his head or tickle his chest so that he does not get overexcited. Praising has to be done with care. Keep the tone of the voice low and warm, the words do not matter too much, but *good* or *clever* when praising, and *bad* or *no* when scolding, are key words always.

Broad- and high-jumping is not difficult. However, all exercise of this sort should be postponed until the dog's physique has fully matured. Run with the dog, and using your voice and the leash, guide him over the hurdles with you alongside.

SALLY ANNE THOMPSON

When you graduate to a hurdle that is too high for you to go over easily, step to the side just as you reach it and let the dog sail over by himself. At this point, you should be using an eight or ten foot leash (a light rope will do). Give him enough slack to jump but keep the line taut enough to correct him if necessary.

Once he has learned hurdle jumping, it can be combined with the retrieve. He should leap over the hurdle, pick up the object, jump the hurdle on his return, and sit before you until the command "Out!"

Sit

The next useful lesson is the sitting exercise. Your puppy will be approaching five months by the time he has learned this much and in all probability be inclined to wander as his normal canine curiosity develops. So if you teach him to sit it will serve as a basis to the command of "Stay" and will act as a curb to this wandering, making him realize that his place is with you, not with the people next door!

SALLY ANNE THOMPSON

If your dog is to present a smart appearance, teach him to sit straight and never allow him to slop over to the side. Keep his head erect, facing forward.

The best time to teach "Sit" is when your puppy is hungry, perhaps just before meal time. Have a small tasty tidbit in your right hand and hold it slightly above his head. At the same time order, "Kim, Sit," and push gently but firmly on his hindquarters so that he drops his rear and assumes a sitting position. Now be quick with your praise as your right hand delivers the tidbit — *not* when he climbs your leg to grab it but *only* when he is sitting properly. The gestures of right hand up and left hand on his rear will soon form an association of ideas. After that comes the tidbit and praise, and before long he will automatically sit when you raise your right hand and give the command. Remember to reward him with praise even when you discontinue the tidbit.

Stay

We now proceed to "Stay" which is helpful in controlling a house dog and for establishing confidence. Once your dog has learned that when you order him to stay you will never fail to return and reward him with praise and/or the tidbit, he will remain quietly waiting even in unfamiliar places. At this phase of puppyhood he may cry and scratch at doors when left alone. Learning to stay will reassure him, and once he has mastered the command you will be able to leave him at any time in any place. He will never fret then, knowing that you will always return to praise him and make the waiting worthwhile.

Put your puppy in the "Sit" position facing you. Be ready to restrain him in the position with the fingers of the left hand. Now lift your right forefinger and catch his eye. At the same time in a *very* firm voice tell him to "Stay!" using your will to make him obey. Don't move away from him the first time; just keep his interest lively with voice and your look. The next time, once he is sitting, you can move back a couple of feet while he sits still. Little by little lengthen the "staying" time until finally you can go outside the door and find him patiently waiting on your return. This may take two weeks to accomplish but you must never weaken and call the dog *to you.* Always return *to him* and give him the expected praise with a quiet voice. Now you are ready to start combining these three exercises into a series with a practical purpose. It will take more time and a lot more patience but you can now teach your puppy to sit and stay while you throw the chamois skin ahead. You can also teach him to return to the sitting position when he has the skin in his mouth. When he is moving

"Sit — Stay!" With the puppy in the "Sit" position facing you, lift your right forefinger and attract his attention. At the same time, in a *very* firm voice tell him to "Stay," using your will to make him obey.

on the leash at your left side you can train him to sit when you stop. The success of your training begins with these first lessons. Dogs are essentially like small children. As a child is formed in its first seven years, a dog is formed in its first six months. Be firm and consistent. Use his name and *one* command. Remember that dogs are highly practical and will seek easy methods to obtain full results with the least trouble or discomfort to themselves — in other words, short cuts to success!

We are all familiar with canine blackmail — barking or crying until they get food at the table or in the kitchen, or refusing to eat until you hand feed them and make a lot of fuss. But you must steel yourself against it. Show your dog that your will is the stronger and that by obeying you and doing things your way he gets praise and comfort and that if he disobeys and follows his own inclinations he receives a

"Stand—Stay!" Here a hand signal is being used in conjunction with the command so that the dog will remain in position while the handler walks away. The same principles are used as in teaching him to "Sit—Stay." The dog must remain standing motionless until released by the trainer's command.

reprimand and correction. This should never vary. A German Shepherd with his wonderful brain power will soon decide that it is easier and more comfortable to obey!

We intend to discuss this business of praising and reprimanding a little more fully now since it is by using these aids fairly that you instill confidence in your dog. If you always have the same reactions, use the same methods, and maintain a calm attitude, your dog will feel secure knowing that when he does certain things you will never fail to respond in *exactly the same* way. Thus he will feel happy and relaxed in the safe little world created by his trust in you.

We mentioned earlier that the tap of a rolled up newspaper was useful to correct a misbehaving puppy. This is quite unsuited to training, however, and so is any form of chastisement with the hand. We repeat once more: the hand is for guiding and caressing . Never hit your dog or threaten him with the hand or you will make him "hand-shy," a pitiful state of affairs.

It is poor thinking for a trainer to imagine that he can scare his dog into obeying him or to keep him from disobeying through fear. Be quick with instant praise or discipline so that the dog associates the deed with your reaction. One cannot teach good behavior just by scolding for bad behavior. The dog must feel the warmth of your praise when he is trying to please even if he succeeds only in small measure, just as he must learn that he gets a scolding and the restraint of your guiding hand when he goes wrong or is inattentive.This guidance with the hand is the real corrective when it is combined with the repeated command in a firmer voice with a bit of "edge" on it to convey to the dog that your will is *not* bending to his. Therefore will he please get on and do as he is bid! To illustrate this point: when you order your dog to sit and he doesn't, you must at once pass your hands along his back to his rear end with enough pressure to position him properly, repeating the command at the same time. Then, when he is sitting correctly, be just as quick with your praise: "Good Kim, clever dog." *Never, never* end a lesson with a correction or you will soon have a reluctant pupil.

Another point to remember is that no matter how furious you may feel at your dog's conduct, you must not scold him or correct him when he returns to you, or he will end up by refusing to come when called. Go to him and correct him if you will, but if he returns to you of his own free will or when you call he must be praised no matter how you feel. The longer your dog lives with you the more his love will require this sense of security when returning to you, so do not risk spoiling it in a moment of impatience. We say this with some feeling, having recently left a puppy in the charge of a well-meaning but uninformed friend who chased after him when he refused to return, scolded him when he was finally caught and left us with six months of hard and anxious work to alter his way of thinking!

Talk to your dog too. He will soon learn from the inflection in your voice what you expect of him when he is with you, and be ready to cooperate. I like to take one or two of our dogs with me in the car when I go shopping or visiting, so when I'm getting ready to leave I casually mention that "Hansel" and "Gretel" must go and lie down (they'll get a tidbit for consolation) and that "Kim" is to go with me this time. There are drooping tails and woeful looks, of course, but from the tone of my voice they are prepared and sometimes even trot off to their kennel and begin gnawing a bone.

Their cries of "Welcome home" when I return show that they hold no ill-feeling and serve as a constant reminder that we should never show resentment toward our dogs for their former misdoings.

To sum up, immediate response and consistency are the keys to good dog training. Never allow a lapse of time between the dog's behavior and your reaction to it. For if you are slow in responding, he will be slow in learning. Therefore, obedience and good efforts are always followed by quiet, warm praise; disobedience entails firm discipline and correction. But never give your dog "punishment" — he is not a criminal!

Heel

You read in Chapter VI how to give your young puppy his first lessons on leash. He will have already become accustomed to his slip chain collar and to walking around the yard or garden with you. Clip on his leash and stand with the dog seated at your left side. Hold the leash well up in your right hand in a position comfortable to yourself, with your left hand fondling the dog's ears or neck to keep him close to your left knee. Then with a clear command, "Heel, Kim," and a tap on your left leg, step off quickly with the left foot, giving the lead a sharp tug with your right hand but release it at once, ready to give another tug if he pulls ahead or lags behind. Praise quickly and quietly if he follows, and then stop and start all over again.

Never allow him to maintain continual pressure on the lead or you will make no headway at all. The success of heel work lies in the art of using the lead in quick tugs to gain the dog's attention and to urge him on in the right direction. But these tugs must be followed by instant release of the leash so that the slip chain slackens. As it

"Heel!" Start the exercise with the dog seated in the "heel" position at your left side. Say cheerfully and clearly, "Heel!" and with a pat of your hand on your left leg, step off quickly with the left foot, giving the leash a sharp tug with your right hand.

The success of heel work lies in the art of using the leash in quick tugs to gain the dog's attention and to urge him on in the right direction. These tugs must be followed by instant release of the leash to slacken the slip chain.

Hold him back each time he tries to pass you, while repeating the command, "Heel!"

slackens come your words of encouragement, "Good Kim, that's right."

Bring him round the back of your legs and make him sit at your left side again, before repeating the exercise. Always cheer him with a little scratch on his chest or behind the ears to reassure him, and if he is boisterous or too playful be a bit firmer next time. Make the lessons

When you have the dog heeling in a straight line, begin a few turns. Just before you make a left turn, get the dog's attention with a " Heel!", and at the same time tighten up with your left hand, held out from your body to keep him from bumping into you. Turn on your left foot, bringing the right foot around in the new direction. If he tangles into you, say, " Heel!", thump him with your knee, and this, with a jerk of the leash, should remind him what to do.

141

short ones of, say, ten minutes each time, and always return him to his kennel or sleeping quarters to rest with a tidbit and caress.

Some dogs are very slow starters at training. Many of our steadiest workers have been slow to learn in the initial stages just as some of our most brilliant scholars began as dunces at school. You must allow time for the ideas to sink in and by following the same pattern each time the dog will soon realize the sequence of events: the slip chain on, the leash clipped on, the position at your left, the caress and praise, then the brisk movement and command, the simultaneous jerk on the lead, your right hand well up in control of the lead, and the left patting the dog or tapping your left leg to attract and encourage

In making a right turn, the dog has much farther to travel. Turn on your right foot, swing your left, and say " Heel!", circling the dog around on a taut leash.

SALLY ANNE THOMPSON

him in position. Then, before either of you are bored or tired he is back at ease, rewarded with praise and some favorite morsel of food.

We have sometimes found that a passage or corridor is a useful place to start heel work for by crowding him to one wall the dog has no chance to stray or pull ahead, but we like to get outside as soon as understanding has been established since this is where control is vital and where he must learn to concentrate on his training.

When the dog is heeling well in a straight line begin a few turns to left and right. Always get him really close to your left leg by the usual encouraging pat and word and an exaggerated rotary motion of the leash in the required direction as the turn is about to be made. Some trainers speed up a bit just before the turns so that the dog is alert and attentive for the change of direction.

You will always, of course, start your heel work with the dog in a sitting position and accustom him to it with the left hand pressure on his back down to the rear, commanding him to take this position every time you stop. Your right hand can lift his chin up meanwhile to check him and keep his attention concentrated on you, but release it before you give the command to start off again. He will thus be well on the way to mastering his exercises of "Sit" and "Stay" since we presume you have already taught him these rudiments as we suggested earlier.

The first lesson was the sitting position with the dog in front of you and the tidbit in your right hand; the next, his heel work lessons beginning and ending with a sit, and you now should teach him to sit in any position by concentrating on this phase for a while. Put on his slip chain and collar and give him the command to sit and keep him there while you reward him with praise. If he moves, scold him and return him to the sitting position with a sharp downward press on his hindquarters, praising him only when he remains sitting. Keep the voice low and praise quietly so that he is not so excited as to stir. When you have the dog at your side and as you use pressure to position him to sit, edge him towards you with the left hand. If you push him sideways from you he will later on be penalized for a crooked sit. You must work on this exercise for some time until he is reliable, as the next is the "Stay" when your dog remains in the "Sit" until you free him by whatever you intend using "All right, Kim," "Free now, Kim," Handlers use quite a range of expressions for this, but whatever command you choose stick with it since changing it will only confuse him.

His heel work lessons begin and end with a "Sit!" If he moves, scold him and return him to the sitting position with a sharp downward press on his hindquarters, praising him only when he remains sitting.

The main point is that the dog remains in this position until *you* return to him. Be careful not to gesture or use your voice in a way that it will seem to give him the cue to come to you. A young and inexperienced dog is always eager to get back to his owner and security, so be a bit cool with him. He may wonder why you are cool, but he will soon recognize your attitude as an indication that he is to stay until you return to him. You will be using the index finger of your raised left hand to gain the attention of the dog seated in front of you, as mentioned before, with the leash in your right hand.

Each time you stop, the dog should sit alongside you. Some trainers prefer to give a command each time, while others teach the dog to respond automatically at each halt. The dog should be alert and eagerly awaiting the next command.

Tell him to stay in a low and purposeful voice, putting him into position if necessary. Step back a pace before raising the finger and catch his eye when giving the command. Count ten silently and release him. Try again until you can count twenty before he gets restless. By the end of two or three lessons he will sit for two or three minutes without restraint, but you must be really businesslike in returning him to position if he moves. Don't confuse him with words. Just give the command with his name *once* and use the leash and your hands to get him sitting without another word. One need not be harsh but a *firm* jerk on the leash and a quick and definite hold on him until he stays quietly will indicate that you intend to be obeyed.

When your dog seems restless or ill at ease at being forced to sit, pet, encourage and reassure him. A willing worker is a better worker.

SALLY ANNE THOMPSON

When a dog that has learned to heel on leash precisely is taken off leash he will respond automatically. Many trainers like to encourage their dogs — particularly in the early stages — by speaking soothingly to them as they walk, repeating the commands and patting their left legs to remind them of the proper position. In the villages of Germany, where leash laws are not strict, it is a marvelous sight to see a man walk down the street with his Shepherd " at heel" and following his every movement like a great ghost.

Repeated commands in either a very loud or a pleading tone are useless, and if you nag your dog he will soon become bored, reducing your efforts to nothing. When training, both handler and dog have much to learn and good results depend on cooperation. If your dog's reponse is poor, ask yourself if you were up to the mark that day; he is very much a part of you now. Naturally, in the early lessons you will have to devise ways to hold his attention. Hower, one command for each action is your goal. The quicker you are with the leash and your hands to control and indicate your requirements, the quicker you will be able to dispense with extra commands in the early stages.

When you have your dog sitting steady for a couple of minutes, drop his lead quietly and turn your back on him with a last command of " Kim, stay." Count ten and turn around quietly before returning to his side. If this is successful you can begin to walk a few paces with your back turned. Always return so that he is on your left side, and finally, in the following lessons, circle your dog, with him ending up on your left.

When you start the next phase — leaving him alone while you disappear from view — it is a good plan to have someone time how long he remains in position. Then you can gauge your return, knowing the limit of his patience in the early stages. Keep to that until he is entirely confident that you will return before extending the period of your absence. If he becomes inattentive during these lessons — and they do require concentration without action — give him a minute or two of brisk heel work before returning to the " Stay." This will freshen him up and lessen the tedium of the inactive periods of sitting still; once again, you have only to recall your own childhood and the punishment of being made to sit still, even for five minutes — it seemed endless!

Down

You are now ready to teach your dog " Down," and from this you will progress to the " Down — Stay" which is much like " Sit — Stay." We favor the use of our own method for teaching this exercise, and this is how we do it. Walk him on the lead, come to a smart halt and have him sit beside you on command. Then kneel beside him, pass your left hand over his body, take his left leg in your hand, reach forward, take his right leg in your right hand and ease him downwards by lifting his front feet until he is lying comfortably beside you, not forgetting a

There are several ways to teach your dog "Down!" The author's favorite method involves using your body weight, as shown here.

decisive command, "Kim, down," at the same time.

In this way your dog is halfway to the floor to begin with, and has the reassurance of your arm around him in this unfamiliar posture. He is more likely to accept this new step than he would if the often suggested method of passing the lead under one's shoe and pulling the dog's head down into a rather ungainly position is used—one which may well alarm him at first.

Another method of teaching "Down" is by passing the leash under your instep and pulling on it, while pressing the dog down. The author does not recommend this method.

Still a third method for teaching your dog "Down!" is to first have him "Sit." Then pull his front paws out from under him while pressing down his shoulders and repeating the command.

When your dog is actually lying beside you, gradually release your left hand and press it lightly on his spine, repeating your command. Then release your right hand and try to keep him in position for a few seconds with only your left hand on his back before giving him the command to sit again. Try the exercise again from the beginning, gradually withdrawing your hands until he will stay down with only the pressure on his back. Then finally cease this until he will stay down quietly without restraint for a few minutes.

It may take several days before you can move gradually from beside him, and he is accustomed to remaining down while you are standing up again, and can control him with one ringing clear command, "Down." Now, if all has gone well with the lessons, he will instantly drop at your side. Remember to praise him warmly. This lesson is an important one for his safety in the future, as it will prevent him from walking into danger if he reacts automatically to your clear command, "Down."

Now, if all has gone well with the lessons, he will instantly drop at your side with one ringing clear command, "Down!"

SALLY ANNE THOMPSON

Your dog must remain in the "Down" position when told to "Stay!" Hold the leash in one hand, and have the other ready to check him if he moves. The important thing is to make the correction before the dog has time to get to his feet.

A well-trained dog will remain in the "Down" position even when someone steps back and forth over him.

SALLY ANNE THOMPSON

Regardless of where he is and whether he is on or off leash, the well-trained animal will immediately drop in response to the palms-down gesture and command of " Down!"

To re-call your dog, bring your right hand diagonally across your body, ending up at the left shoulder, in a broad sweeping gesture and command "Come!" This should first be taught while using a long leash which can be tugged if he does not respond promptly.

SALLY ANNE THOMPSON

The dog, when re-called, should come straight to the handler and "Sit" immediately in front. This dog is not sitting squarely on his haunches, a position which in obedience competition would be penalized.

The next step is to give the command "Go to heel!" Step back slightly and the dog will rise and follow you. As he does so, bring him around to your left side, circle him as on a pivot, and give the command "Sit!"

The exercise is now completed with the dog seated at your left side. Were this actual obedience competition, the dog would maintain this position until the judge signaled completion.

Food Refusal

A word now about tricks. Some of these are developed from the obedience exercises and form a little relief from the daily training. Moreover, as most dogs love to show off, they help to maintain keenness and interest in work. One of the most useful tricks — if you can call it a trick (for guard dogs it's a must) — is the refusal of food from a stranger. Once you have taught this, you will have to make a firm rule in your family not to offer tidbits at any time, or your lessons and the usefulness of this discipline will be lost. Remember that we are dealing here with strong conflicting instincts in the dog — on the one hand his desire to please and obey his owner, to ignore or distrust others, and on the other, his habit of working for a tasty morsel as a reward along with praise. Food is good to his way of thinking, whether it is offered by his owner or by a stranger.

SALLY ANNE THOMPSON

One of the most useful tricks, if you can call it a trick — for guard dogs it's a must — is refusal of food from a stranger.

Pretending to be dead is another effective trick. With your dog lying down, roll him over with one hand and scratch his chest and belly with the other, while giving the command "Die for your country — Stay!"

So we must play on his heartstrings and loyalty to teach him that this time he is to work to please his owner and no one else. Prepare a tidbit. Have your dog in the sitting position, give him the command to stay, and stand facing him. Then catch his eyes and look hard at him, at the same time uttering the deterrent word of "No" or "Leave" in a low intense voice to emphasize that it is a warning *not* to touch the food you are holding on the palm of your hand in front of him. Stop him from coming to sniff or eat the food with another warning word firmly given, and try to control him for five or ten seconds. Then say, "Okay, Kim," or "Take it, Kim" and allow him to devour the tidbit. You must offer the food with alternate hands, controlling with the other, or your dog may associate the command of warning with one hand and not the other.

Next put the food on a plate and use the same procedure. Afterwards, try putting it on the floor or a low table, and finally when he has grasped the idea that he must wait for your permission to eat, seek the cooperation of another handler to tempt him with dainties while you give the commands. Then, as the dog progresses you can lower your tone until it is as faint as a whisper, until, in the end, he will understand just by the quick stern glance you give him and not attempt to eat any food, however delicious, even when you are a long way off.

This is not a difficult trick but it requires some persistence and a firm voice and eye control to bring success and the polish which makes it look so natural. Praise him quietly when he turns away from the food at your warning command, as you will want him to remain in position for another attempt. As well as being a "party piece" this trick will prevent him from accepting doped or poisoned food from any thieves who may invade your home.

"Die for Your Country!"

Pretending to be dead is another effective trick that can be developed from the "Down" position. When your dog is lying down, roll him over with one hand and scratch his chest and belly with the other, instructing him with the command, "Die for your Country — Stay." When you command him, "Alive, Kim", use an excited tone and rattle his slip chain or leash so that he barks and gives the impression of returning to life. Most dogs bark with pleasure when they hear their lead and collar jingling, and all dogs adore having their bellies scratched. So you can teach this easy trick just by appealing to his sense of pleasure; it is one which he will always enjoy. It has its value too. One of our good friends who lives alone had an unknown visitor who insisted on entering the house, but with great presence of mind she commanded her dog to "die." When the intruder was well inside the door, she called, "Alive," and made a dash for the telephone while the dog cornered the man who would otherwise have escaped.

To train your Shepherd for "Scent Discrimination," have an assistant cut a broom handle that you have never touched into three-inch lengths and give you several. Handle just a few so that your scent will be attached to them. Drop these, together with a number of lengths which you have not handled, into the training area and have your dog select the ones with your scent on them. This is a very effective trick, particularly if you have the lengths of different colors so that the spectators can distinguish between the right and wrong ones.

These exercises and many more have been described by expert obedience trainers in countless books. However we have approached them from the beginner's point of view and hope that your interest has been stimulated and sustained by our methods. There are training classes and dog schools where one can learn more advanced work, or even send a dog for instruction, but these basic lessons are essential. The most brilliant performers began with them, just as you and your dog have done, so do not feel " small". or discouraged when witnessing some cleverly trained dog. It all started with a small puppy, a pair of gentle hands, a firm quiet voice and a slip chain, and was accomplished by long hours of repetition and a full measure of tireless enthusiasm and patience.

But make it all fun, treat it as a hobby and recreation. A dog's time with us is comparatively short so it is up to us to make his few years happy in return for the devotion he gives and the wonderful memories he leaves when, alas, he is no more.

Problem Dogs

We are so jealous of the good reputation of all German Shepherd Dogs that we want you all to agree that untrustworthy traits have no place at all in anybody's home, and that, if you do have an animal that is fierce or unreliable in its reactions it must be destroyed for everyone's safety. Do not wait until there has been a nasty accident before putting the unfortunate dog to sleep; it should be done as soon as the danger is realized. There is no shame attached to it. Criminal characteristics occur in all breeds at times, just as they do in all human families! The important thing is to see that nobody suffers, and, as a child or an unsuspecting friend could be attacked by a bad tempered dog, the only reasonable action to take is to prevent it from happening.

There are many dogs that have faulty character or temperament but a good disposition; this is to say that while they lack courage or stability they are not fierce or uncertain in their reactions. These animals can usually be accommodated in homes with understanding people who do not require a working or guard dog and would have patience with such a reticent companion.

Dogs go through a " teenage" phase much like young people. With bitches the change in their character usually comes when they are about six to nine months old, the expected time of their first season.

Then they may become shy of strangers and " jumpy." They may also become very choosy over their food for a while. It is unwise to force them into any new experiences at this time. Let them free in a closed run and give a tonic for a week or two which you should ask your veterinarian to prescribe.

A few simple obedience lessons with reassuring praise may help the return of the dog's confidence, and once the heat season is over you will usually find that everything is back to normal.

A dog between nine and fifteen months is sometimes a problem because he is reaching his maximum growth and needs all his strength for development. Don't overtax him with strenuous training or use him at stud more than a couple of times to prove him. He can have the tonic too, and plenty of fresh raw meat with an egg yolk added daily to build him up. Plenty of rest and some simple obedience training will help him. Take him about with you to see the world on foot and by car so that his mind develops at the same pace as his body.

A dog that is shy with strangers or one that jumps at noises in the street can often be helped by firm handling and much understanding. If you will sit quietly with the dog at a busy bus or railroad station for a short time each day he will soon learn to ignore people and noises, unless he is pathologically nervous, and in that case the unhappy dog should be destroyed. Shy dogs suffer torture; it is really unkind to keep one alive. There is also the fear-biter—a timid dog who, if approached by a stranger, will fly out and bite and then run away or, alternatively, run away and sneak back to bite from behind. Such a dog has no place in anyone's house.

At the first sign of recalcitrance, have the dog's ears and teeth checked. Many animals have been blamed for bad dispositions when an aching or decayed tooth or an ear full of canker mites was the real cause of trouble.

Kennelling a timid dog with one of bold and fearless temperament is often helpful. Dogs are great imitators. But the bold one should be the older, or the shy one may be a bad influence.

The German Shepherd as a Guard Dog

Many people purchase a German Shepherd as a protector and guardian for the home. While there is no doubt that the breed is admirably suited for this purpose we must also bear in mind that there are responsibilities involved in training such a dog.

From the legal point of view, the owner is responsible for the actions of his dog, and therefore any dog which is trained to attack must be so controlled that he does not become a menace to innocent passers-by. From the ethical and moral point of view, you must remember that it is extremely nerve racking to have a visitor or a tradesman stand or sit rigidly in your home with an apparently ferocious dog glaring at him and growling at every movement. Therefore, if you are to utilize your dog for this purpose he must be so trained as to be under your control at all times and have a clear understanding of his relationship to people.

A German Shepherd will, while still quite a small puppy, bark at and show interest in strangers, particularly if you excite him by your tone of voice and manner. As for example, when someone walks towards the door you say excitedly, "Who's there? Who's at the door?" Repeat it several times in an excited tone of voice and the dog will get up to investigate. When the knock comes, you repeat in a high pitched voice, "Who's there?" and clap your hands several times. It will not take too long before the dog will bark a few times, and when he does this you praise him and possibly offer a tidbit. It will not be long before he barks at everyone approaching the door in order to get his reward and praise.

At this point start teaching him control. Allow him two or three barks and then say, "Good boy, quiet!" Hold his mouth closed with one hand while repeating, "Quiet," until he gets the idea. When you open the door insist that he sit to one side and if he growls or barks, repeat, "Quiet!"

Do not permit him to approach strangers without your permission. Instead, make him "sit" until released on command. As we have seen earlier in this chapter, he must also be trained not to accept food from strangers.

The training of an attack dog should be left to a highly skilled and experienced trainer, as in the hands of an amateur such a dog can be as deadly as a gun.

Your greatest protection is that once your dog has learned to *bark* at the approach of a stranger or a prowler, any intruder will know that his presence is being announced to the neighborhood; he will not be anxious to enter a home once he knows there is a German Shepherd in it, as the breed's reputation for strength, courage and protectiveness is legendary.

Outdoor shows are usually held in the spring of the year and are a delight both to spectators and participants. This scene is a show in England, but it would be recognizable anywhere in the world.

XI Dog Shows

The exhibition of well-bred and beautifully conditioned and presented dogs is a thrilling and absorbing sport. It can give endless pleasure and interest to those who indulge in it, although, as in all sports and hobbies, it is well to remember at all times that *it is a sport* and that good fortune and bad alike play their part. One must not take showing as a matter of life and death and spoil the fun with a too serious, or, worse still, an entirely commercial outlook.

Showing any dog is an expensive business and German Shepherds may be the top bracket. If you are not young and/or in very good physical condition for the long gaiting at fast speeds, you will have to engage a handler — usually a well paid professional — to exhibit your dog for you, and this adds considerably to the cost of exhibiting.

As ours is a natural looking breed no great grooming preparation is needed. A Terrier or a Poodle, for example, has to be trimmed and clipped by experts to look its best in the ring.

However, we are at one disadvantage with the very " natural" dog. There is no thick coat to disguise his faults or enhance his virtues, nor will clever preparation be of any help. Whatever he possesses, or lacks, is all there to be seen plainly by the discerning eye. This makes it of the greatest importance that the German Shepherd should be in perfect physical condition, healthy and sound and well disciplined when presented in the ring if he is to create a good impression. To accomplish this requires many hours of concentrated effort.

We have what is classified in dogdom as a working breed, which means that the dog should be kept in hard physical condition with firm muscles, particularly in back line, with short well-muscled feet,

A Swedish Champion German Shepherd. Study this picture and then compare it with the show dogs in America. Although the differences are minor, they are quite noticeable.

AKE WINTZELL

and have a gleaming dense coat of correct length and texture indicating that he is in good health. So when you know the date of your show (which will be announced weeks beforehand) start giving your dog extra walks if he has put on weight or grown soft during winter or bad weather. Give him extra fat in his diet to help condition his coat. Work on his coat with good firm brushes — the whale bone "dandy" brush used for grooming horses is most satisfactory. This can be washed and dried quickly after use, and when the weather or other circumstances make bathing out of the question, extra grooming with these big clean brushes will keep your dog immaculate.

Attend to his ears (see my chapter on Grooming). Also see that his nails are reasonably short. A well-exercised dog should have an arched and closely knit foot. With normal running at exercise and play he will usually keep his nails worn down, and so use the foot correctly and in conjunction with his pastern. I discussed nail trimming in my chapter on Grooming. Clip them well ahead of the show date so if a toe is cut accidentally it will have plenty of time to heal.

Whether your dog is in or out of coat at show time is largely a matter of luck. If "in" you can clean him with your brushes, or if the weather permits, give him a bath a week before the show and spend the following days combing and brushing to get the coat sleek and shining. If you have the misfortune to pick a show in the middle of his shedding period, comb and brush away all tufts and loose hairs. If these are left on the dog they only accentuate his condition, and while every judge prefers a dog in full bloom, many do not penalize for being out of coat if the dog is clean and hard. Check his mouth too, and if the teeth are discolored, rub with a soft piece of old linen dipped in peroxide of hydrogen (3%) and then in powdered pumice, or use baking soda, but without peroxide. With a prick eared breed, the condition of the ears is most noticeable so these must be cleaned inside with a little sweet almond oil or one of the many commercial products specially formulated for this. Remove the wax and grease carefully. Prevent any liquids from getting into the base of the ear and causing irritation by inserting a small plug of cotton before starting the operation.

Comb the bushy hair of his " pants" and make sure that there is no dried excrement, sponging them with cool water if necessary.

Most of the foregoing preparations are part of the daily care of the dog, and it may only remain for you to check on all points and give a little extra polish the day before the show. You can then step confidently into the ring with an immaculate animal knowing that he will gain full marks for condition, however he may be faulted otherwise. We have a saying in our kennel that "Dogs are made in heaven but their condition is made by us!"

Today, with the extensive use of antibiotics and the highly perfected injections given against the dreaded killer diseases, we are not so concerned about precautions at shows as we once were. However, we still like to swab the dog's mouth out with one of the many special disinfectants for mouth hygiene, and we do this *before* and *after* the show. If you have small un-inoculated puppies back home in the kennel, keep an old towel soaked in disinfectant and water in a thick plastic bag and when you reach home spread it out on the garage floor; stand on it yourself to sterilize your shoes and stand your dog on it so that his feet are cleansed of any show taint. Try to keep the show dog away from his companions for 24 hours and positively keep him away from a litter of small puppies. If you are at all worried by rumors of infection at the show, take the dog's temperature night and morning for two days so that you can alert your veterinarian at the first sign of trouble.

Ringcraft

If you decide to engage a professional handler he will want your dog in his kennels for a period before the show to train him in ringcraft or show presentation.

If, however, you intend to exhibit the dog yourself, you must give him lessons on posing and gaiting, and familiarize him with moving around in company with other dogs, and also with being handled by a total stranger since a judge will examine him carefully.

Training given in puppyhood will be helpful. You will also by this time—if you are show minded—have joined your area German Shepherd Club and have taken part in a few matches to accustom yourself and your dog to show procedure. Nothing written about showing a dog can help you half so much as a few practical hints demonstrated by an expert; this is where your club comes in. Ask the best handlers if they can spare a few minutes to put you right with your dog. German Shepherd breeders are invariably helpful to novice owners (whatever their attitude may be if and when you start taking

Your dog will show at his best if he is familiar with the handler and there is a common bond of confidence. This gives him a feeling of security which will reflect itself in an improved ring manner.

all the ribbons!). Some clubs have classes for ringcraft. Go to them in a relaxed frame of mind and train yourself always to enter the ring calmly. Whatever feelings you display travel straight down the leash to your dog, and if you fuss and fidget so will he. Many dogs in the ring are faulted for nerves which are more properly faults of their owners.

We favor the manner of presentation used in Germany. The Germans teach their dogs to move ahead the full length of the leash. This gives them an alert, independent appearance which appears to owe nothing to actual handling. It can only be achieved by long hours

Champion Leo of Llanyravon being shown in the natural, or German, method of showing. The dog is taught to move ahead the full length of the leash.

of practice. It seems to emphasize German Shepherd character by the freedom of movement, the natural head carriage and fearless expression which says clearly "Look at me, I'm doing this all by myself!" It also indicates to the judge that the dog is well mannered and can be allowed to move without close restraint, and that his temperament is so bold that he does not have to be coaxed out from behind his handler for display.

It is true to say that the more a dog is maneuvered or "handled" in the ring — particularly on a tightly stretched leash "strung up" (like a Boxer and similar breeds with arched necks) — the more one's suspicions are raised that something is being covered up. While "stringing up" may help give more reaching appearance to a short or stocky neck, it also prevents the dog from putting the normal pressure on his front legs and standing "four square." This destroys his balance and gives him a straight-in-shoulder look. These are not the only unfortunate impressions that are created by the tight leash. When the bulk of the dog's weight is transferred to his hind legs he will drop down and assume a groveling attitude which is as unnatural as it is ugly, totally belying the alert courageous temperament of the German Shepherd.

When you have taught your dog to stand correctly, make him hold the stance while you step back the length of the leash and a friend, acting as judge, examines the dentition or runs his hands along the back in preparation to testing him for "entirety." This is one of the most difficult things you will ever have to teach your dog as the testicles are his most sensitive and vulnerable spot. An experienced judge will gently run a hand down his back or pat the hindquarters with one hand, meanwhile carefully exploring the scrotum to feel if both testicles are properly descended. It is a disqualifying fault if one (monorchidism) or both (cryptorchidism) are undescended. So get a few friends to cooperate from time to time by rehearsing this test with your dog in the show stance. Always keep a firm grip on his slip collar at these times; if pain is caused he may take retaliatory action. You can give a helping hand to a friend's dog with this problem in return; it is one all dog exhibitors have to face.

The next ordeal is examination of the mouth and there are several good ways (and even more bad ones) of going about this preparation. Perhaps the best way is to place your dog in the sitting position and then straddle his back so that your knees are on either side. This will insure control while both your hands are occupied with his mouth. It will also give him confidence. Many dogs dislike having their mouths examined. We sometimes think that this antipathy is caused by careless overhandling of the mouth when the puppy is teething and the gums are swollen and sensitive. So do not be in a hurry to teach him this exercise, and be sure that his gums are not inflamed at the time of the lesson. Otherwise, you may make him difficult about showing his mouth for all time.

So, with your dog in position, tilt his nose upwards with your hand under his chin and part the lips with your other hand so that the judge can clearly see the "bite" — the top teeth resting on and even slightly overlapping the lower set in the desired "scissor bite." If you are exhibiting a puppy you may not be required to show more than the bite since his pre-molars and after-molars may not come through until he is almost a year old; indeed we have heard of cases where the pre-molars did not come through until 18 months. For the mature dog, however, you must first lift the top lip, then turn down the lower one at each side of the mouth in turn so that the pre-molars can be seen and the canines examined. Keep your own head behind the dog's head so that the judge can have a clear view. It is no exaggeration to say that half of all exhibitors lean forward and examine the teeth themselves, thus obscuring the view!

The extent to which your dog will be penalized for any missing teeth (usually the pre-molars) depends somewhat on the judge's personal attitude to the fault, unless he is a German or continental judge. He may count each tooth and follow the ruling that if more than one pre-molar (either upper or lower) is missing, the dog cannot receive the classification of " Excellent." Dirty teeth may bring you a bad mark on condition but teeth discolored from Distemper, although not often seen today, are not really a fault but actually a blemish left from illness, to be considered as a misfortune but no more.

Teach your dog to stand naturally, with his front feet set straight and not too close together, one hind leg forward and slightly under the body in the classic stance.

If you intend to show your dog, teach him to hold still for examination. Have your
friends handle and run their hands over him to accustom him to the touch of a judge.

You must now pose your dog — "set him up" is the expression
commonly used. You will have taught him at home to stand naturally
with his front feet set straight and not too close together, one hind leg
forward and slightly under the body in the classic stance. How this is
achieved depends largely on the dog and how he reacts to his handler.
Some will allow their limbs to be moved into position and remain like
statues during examination; others are more spirited and may strike
a natural pose and remain there for a couple of minutes, then move
around and have to be re-positioned if the judge has not completed
his examination.

Most exhibitors use a tidbit to keep the dog on his toes and
attentive during the stance. This is good provided that the bait is not
held above the dog's normal line of vision. If it is held high, up goes
the head to strain after the food and the shoulder line is altered and
straightened and the dog is generally thrown off balance. Always
remember that the German Shepherd Dog is a forward reaching
animal; the head is not carried high like a hunting dog scenting birds.
His characteristic determination is shown by the easy forward
reaching neck with the head carried not high or tilted up but level,
with the chin on the same line as the base of the neck, especially in
movement. One of the tricks used in showing is to feed your dog early

on the day before the show and give him nothing but liquids afterwards so that he is hungry and eager for the tidbit and unusually keen and alert. Do not keep him off liquids, however, or he will look drawn up in loin which may spoil his underline.

The judge may now run his hands over the dog feeling the layback of shoulder and testing the firmness of back, also looking into the coat for texture and density of undercoat. There is so much to be looked at during the three or four minutes your dog is actually on show! Without engaging in conversation, your judge may tell you what he wants you to do in the way of posing and gaiting, and you are at liberty to ask what he requires of you and the dog by saying, " Do you want me to stand him (move him, etc.) now?" If you have to ask questions, it is better to address your ring steward who is well versed in show business. Don't talk loudly to your dog either; keep calm and use a low tone to issue commands. A dog's hearing is very sensitive and he will remember his drill better if you speak quietly. Your own attitude may govern his, and if you are tense and nervous he may well have similar reactions.

After each individual examination it is usual for the dog to be gaited round the ring, and to be sent up and down, or across the ring and back, to assess the track and the firmness of shoulders and hocks. Move your dog in a straight line so that a true assessment can be made, moving diagonally may be accidental or it may be a clever maneuver to disguise an action which weaves or falters. In any case the experienced judge's suspicions will be aroused and he will send you out to do it again. Take your time moving around the ring. It is your " moment of truth" and it is up to you to make the most of it. Let your dog move freely on a loose leash. In horsey language " give him his head." There is no finer sight than a German Shepherd gaiting at his own speed without restraint.

When the judge has completed the individual examinations he will have the whole class gait around the ring together. Now it is a different story. Your dog must never be allowed to overrun the dog ahead, nor lag behind and cause the one following to stumble and be handicapped. Let him move on a loose leash, by all means, but sideways towards the center of the ring away from your left side, and always well away from the other exhibits as good sportsmanship dictates. When the class is halted, be ready to " set your dog up" to refresh the judge's memory so that he can make his comparisons of type and construction.

If you do not gain a ribbon, leave the ring quietly after a word of congratulation to the winner. If there is time after all judging has been completed, ask the reasons for your placing. If, on the other hand, you are awarded a ribbon, accept it thankfully and spare a few words for the loser such as "Your dog looked so well today," or "I was lucky to beat your lovely dog." If you gain a reputation for kind consideration, it will earn you many friends.

MADELEINE PICKUP

Three 3-month-olds playing about a traveling box. This way they will grow accustomed to it long before it is used to take them to a show by car.

Show Hints

You will need a large strongly made hold-all type of bag to carry your show gear which will roughly consist of the following:

Towel	Brush, comb and chamois skin
Drinking bowl	Tidbits
Bench chain	Disinfectant, small size
Entry passes	Brandy, small flask
Pair of loose gloves	Facial tissues

171

We take along a couple of thick newspapers secured by a rubber band to spread on the bench under the rug for comfort and warmth. (These do not have to be carried home afterward when one is tired!) Dogs seldom eat at one-day shows, nor should they be fed in case they may be required in the ring. You can, however, take some meat along or a can of meat (don't forget the can opener). You may also want to take a thermos of coffee and some food for yourself. Food at shows is usually expensive and of varying quality, and it may be that you will not want to leave your exhibit alone on his bench, and there is always the sales angle for your kennel — you should be on hand to answer all inquiries, or prospective business will move to the next bench.

Before you reach the show, stop to walk your dog so that he is comfortable, or he will not show well. While there are exercising rings at the show, some dogs refuse to use them. On arrival, you must pass a veterinary inspection so keep your dog well under control if he is excited. The doctor is not there to be bitten! When he has passed the dog, go at once to your bench and settle him until the judging commences, and allow plenty of time for the final touches.

Wear loose fitting gloves as dog shows are notoriously dirty places, and washrooms can be far away and at outdoor shows somewhat primitive. Brush and comb the dog and give him a last going over with the chamois skin to smooth his coat and make it gleam. Find out when your class will be called and enter the ring promptly when asked to do so. With the many entries at shows today the judge needs everyone's cooperation to finish in time. Moreover, your fellow exhibitors will resent being kept waiting. It is a difficult task to keep a dog on its toes for long periods, and as German Shepherds are frequently judged outside even in cold weather, no one wants to be kept waiting by inattentive entrants.

Traveling

Small dogs usually travel well, large breeds suffer more from travel sickness. The well-sprung rear seat of your car with its sloping angle is unsuitable and uncomfortable for a German Shepherd. If you drive a station wagon, use a thin mattress enclosed in a zip fastened waterproof cover the size of the platform, and cover this with a thin washable blanket. Put thick newspapers on top so that any "distress signals" can be quickly and inoffensively removed when you reach a disposal point. A large teaspoonful of honey melted in warm water can be given with advantage about half an hour before leaving home, or a soupspoonful of powdered dextrose prepared in the same way. Beware of human travel sickness remedies; several of them are unsuited to dogs. If your dog does not respond to the honey or dextrose and a few practice rides of short duration, ask your veterinarian for a tranquilizer. Obviously, one should never feed a dog for at least two hours before a journey begins; even seasoned travelers react badly if they ride too soon after a meal.

If you want to take your German Shepherd in a sedan model car, first remove the rear seat. If you plan to take the dog long distances or have him travel frequently, build a light plywood platform the same shape as the seat so that it fits well back, and attach two strong legs or supports on hinges which will drop and support the front. Cover it with a waterproof cover like that described for the station wagon. Your dog will travel without cramps or discomfort and usually without sickness once he is accustomed to the motion.

We make it a rule to stop and exercise our dogs every 50 miles if traffic is heavy or every 100 miles on a clear road. The stop need not be long, but dogs need to get out and stretch their legs, particularly if they are traveling to a show, otherwise they will arrive stiff-muscled.

There are a number of motorists who claim that travel sickness in both children and dogs can be remedied by trailing a length of strong metal chain from the rear axle of the car so that it makes contact with the ground and breaks the static electricity which builds up in a moving vehicle. It is a harmless remedy worth giving a trial as there is nothing worse than travel-sick animals. There is no doubt that they suffer terribly and need time to settle down afterwards. Show dogs can lose condition from vomiting and subsequent internal disturbances and, naturally, they are hardly ready to give their best if they have an upset stomach.

The best method to condition your puppy is to take him on short trips, and to stop the car and let him out and comfort him as soon as he shows distress. Two or three of these brief trips may well do more to reassure him than any number of pills. Once a dog accepts the car it is hard to keep him out of it!

Some cures have been effected by "kenneling" the dog in the car for short periods while it is left standing in the driveway or garage. Feed him in it or give him a few favorite tidbits so that he associates the vehicle with pleasant things. If he is not inclined to chew or tear up the upholstery, he can be left to sleep in the car for one or two nights. Once he realizes that he can get in and not become travel-sick, it may break the association of ideas which causes the malaise. We have had only a couple of dogs in our lifetime in dogdom who were incurably travel sick, but most were enthusiastic motorists.

Strange to relate, few dogs ever become air sick unless they have been unwisely fed beforehand, nor does a train disturb them if they travel on an empty stomach. Of course this applies only to short trips. A dog traveling long distances must be fed, but light dry meals are best. Send a container of honey or Karo and water with the traveler; it will sustain him if he is disinclined to eat.

If a puppy on his way to a show is inclined to drool and slobber over his front feet and chest, tie a small rough towel round him like a child's bib. Saliva is difficult to remove without washing thoroughly, and it can leave an ugly dark stain on the animal.

Using a traveling box for a German Shepherd is not common, but some breeders prefer to keep a puppy who may be travel sick separated from an older dog. Some feel that puppies travel better in a warm box in winter. If you decide to use one, give ample ventilation but turn the box so that the air holes are not toward the side of the car. Watch that the direct draft from an open window does not blow in on him or he may catch a serious chill or have an attack of conjunctivitis.

Do not allow any dog to lean out of a window while the car is in motion as dogs have no eyelashes to shield the eyes from the wind, and they can be badly affected by dust and exhaust gases. If your dog is an incurable window gazer, have a light wire screen made for the window so that it can be opened for ventilation while he is safely protected.

German Shepherds are so intelligent that you will have no difficulty in believing us when we tell you that one of our bitches taught herself that if she looked out of the rear window of the station wagon she would not be travel sick and happily traveled thousands of miles with her back to the crew and cargo! Another old dog was a speed demon. He would sleep soundly until we reached around 70 m.p.h.; then he would stand up, tail waving, and gaze ahead with bright eyes enjoying the car speed.

Obedience trials are frequently held in conjunction with dog shows. At these trials, which are regulated by the AKC, dogs are tested as to their responsiveness and obedience to commands. Depending on their abilities, degrees are awarded. These tests entitle the successful contestant to the following degrees, which are indicated as suffixes after his name: C.D. (Companion Dog), C.D.X. (Companion Dog Excellent), U.D. (Utility Dog), and, finally, the highest award in obedience, U.D.T. (Utility Dog Tracker). German Shepherds rank consistently high in the number of degrees awarded.

Wendy, owned by Simon and Myrtle Funderburg of Duranburg Shepherd Kennel in California. In the author's opinion, a bitch should not be used for breeding until her third heat, and then she would be nearly two years old. As this breed develops very slowly, she will not have matured fully until this age.

XII   Breeding

Breeding is not really in the novice owner's program, but if you own a dearly loved pet bitch you may wish to perpetuate her lovely qualities. Or again, by this time you may have become so enthralled by the

German Shepherd Dog (and we all know how easy that is!) that you feel you would like to join those who have the thrilling experience of breeding a litter and watching it grow up.

Reproducing such a large breed can be an expensive affair. German Shepherds usually have large litters. Housing and feeding costs a lot. Shipping and advertising costs are high. And if the puppies are not sold within eight or ten weeks, you will be faced with the additional expense of inoculations and will need time for training because the German Shepherd, with his intelligent makeup, cannot just be left in his kennel after the age of twelve weeks. He must get about and see the world or he may become retiring and shy. If you feel equipped to take on all these responsibilities, here is the first hurdle — the choice of a male, known in dog parlance as a stud.

If you have kept in touch with the breeders of your bitch inquire what experiences they have had with her bloodlines and ask them to recommend a suitable mate. You could also attend a few shows and look around for the type of dog whose character and shape you prefer. First of all, type should match type. Then try to work out the heredity so that you do not make the mistake of interbreeding on a line which carries notable faults of conformation or character. Take several opinions before making your choice, remembering that all dogs have some faults and that you are seeking a dog to complement your bitch. One, for example, that carries extra good shoulders if her fault is lack of shoulder angulation, or very well developed hindquarters if her weakness lies there. But do not choose, on any account, a dog with a faulty temperament, however beautiful. This is to court disaster, even if your bitch is very firm in character. The compensation of weakness with strength is the key to successful breeding, but do not forget that character is every bit as important as conformation.

In my opinion a bitch should not be used for breeding until her third heat and then she will be nearly two years old. As this breed matures very slowly, she will not have completed her own development until this age. Carrying a litter of up to a dozen puppies imposes an enormous strain on a bitch and she must be strong and ready for the ordeal. Otherwise, you may have the task of rearing the puppies by hand, if she is not up to the mark at the time of whelping.

We have just mentioned that there may possibly be a litter of twelve puppies. German Shepherds have very large litters frequently; we had seventeen once! Though nature is a generous provider, it does not mean that she meant the poor mother to rear such a large number

When selecting breeders, it is important that the dog (left) be thoroughly masculine and that the female (right) be typically feminine.

of babies. In her wild state the bitch would have her puppies under some bush or in a hole in the ground in the forest, and several would die of cold or exposure or be smothered in the overcrowded bed. Most bitches are equipped to suckle eight puppies and, in our considered opinion, this is the maximum number she should be allowed to rear. Six is even better. A medium sized litter of strong puppies is far less work than a family of ten or twelve that has to be carefully and constantly scrutinized to see that every puppy has had his fill of milk. You may have to supplement this milk by hand feeding. If not, the greedy babies may drain their mother and bring on Eclampsia.

Your veterinarian will dispose of the weakest of the litter after four or five days. This allows time for the very weak ones to die naturally, and for you to reject any with abnormalities, such as a cleft palate or a very pale (or white) color. Euthanasia is performed painlessly by injection. You will, however, be doing the kindest and wisest thing if you put the mother as far away from her family as possible while you and the veterinarian attend to the matter. We have even taken mothers for short rides in the car until everything was calm again.

The Mating

Let us now assume that you have chosen the stud dog and arranged for his service. As soon as your bitch is in season, notify the dog's owner and decide on a date 12 to 14 days ahead so that he will reserve the stud for her. Bitches vary considerably in the dates when they will accept the dog. You will have to test yours with a folded cleansing tissue held against the vulva to find out when the flow diminishes and she starts to "stand" to indicate that she is ready for service. This "stand" is shown by the planting of the feet foursquare and bracing the hindquarters with her tail lifted high over the back or to one side. If you apply the pressure of your hand on her hindquarters she will show pleasure by wagging her tail and whining.

Her state of readiness for the dog lasts about 48 hours normally but there are bitches who will only accept the dog during a few hours of their heat period while others will be willing for a whole week. Matings and studwork are largely trial and error perforce, and the experienced breeder is quite accustomed to the uncertainty of the bitch's mating day. You will, of course, do your best to make certain by checking on her condition daily and informing the dog's owner as early as possible of the time of her impending visit. If not, you may find that another has taken her date.

If you have been using aerosol and chlorophyll deodorants during the bitch's season to discourage unwanted males from visiting her you must stop their use 48 hours before she goes to the dog. Carefully sponge any trace of the repellent off her" pants and petticoats" or the stud dog may be misled into thinking she is not in heat. See that she is well exercised and has defecated before going to the dog. This is very important for her comfort, particularly if she has traveled a long way. So, during the trip, stop and take her out for a walk and let her perform her natural functions.

Take along a length of wide gauze bandage (see Chapter XVII) in case she is reluctant and tries to snap at the dog. His owner will indicate how you can best hold her and help. But if she is uncooperative it is better to muzzle her so that nobody gets bitten, even inadvertently. You will find a detailed discussion of the mating act in the section on Studwork. Always ask the dog's owner for a second service free of charge if the first proves unsuccessful. Should she not produce puppies after 63 days, let him know so that arrangements can be made for her next season. Keep the future mother quiet after the service, and do not offer her cold water to drink nor allow her to urinate for at least one hour.

The Pregnant Bitch

She may not show physical signs of pregnancy for about six weeks — in a deep bodied breed like ours the secret can be kept for a long time! However, increased appetite, drowsiness and in some cases a great show of affection will indicate that her family is on the way.

Food will play an increasingly important role in the daily routine now. As her pregnancy advances she requires two smaller meals of a ration with sufficient calcium.

If you like to fuss, at six weeks, for breakfast give her a small bowl of Cream of Wheat with fresh milk, sweetened with our old friend — honey or Karo.

From six weeks onwards she should have four meals every day — the breakfast of Cream of Wheat being repeated for the last meal at bedtime with the two main meals of $1^1/_2$ to 2 pounds of meat according to her appetite, with a small amount of kibble or dried bread. Do not feed her between meals however much she begs for food and do not give any kind of rich baby foods or "human" nightcap preparations; these are too rich in fats.

Toward the eighth week your expectant mother may go off her food and be very choice about what she will (or will not) eat. Now you can relax the rules a little and give small quantities of her favorite foods — cooked beef for a change, some carefully boned fresh fish with a raw egg yolk, or an egg custard baked with a little honey. *Give no bones after the eighth week.* Some bitches eat normally right up to whelping time while others are difficult and "choosy," so one must be prepared to pamper them a little — always keeping it within limits — we once had an owner who boasted that his dog would eat nothing but canned salmon and chocolate biscuits! The golden rule is never to introduce your dog to such dainties; then neither he nor you will be tempted to use them in his diet. If you don't want to go to all this fuss, feed the bitch a good, wholesome prepared dog food with 15 % added fat. This will provide all essential nutrients, save much time and money. Feed her all she will eat without becoming overweight.

Now is the time to attend to the teats. These should be sponged in lukewarm water with some antiseptic soap, rinsed with clear water and thoroughly dried; afterwards massage each one with a small quantity of olive oil. This will prevent cracks and sores which could cause pain when the puppies start to nurse. Do this massage daily now, and don't be alarmed if a few drops of milk appear at any time after the 58th day. This is quite normal. It also indicates that puppies can arrive at any time, usually within 48 hours. At about the 60th day we clip back the dense fur of her " panties" around the vulva and from the under side of her tail about half way to the tip. This makes for a cleaner whelping, and it is easier to see when a puppy gets stuck as it sometimes does. Twenty-four hours before labor there will be a drop in her temperature.

If the future mother is not already sleeping in her whelping quarters, she should be introduced to them not later than ten days prior to the expected event. It should be in a room or a large kennel where you can stand up, or you will be uncomfortable when feeding and attending to mother and babies during the coming weeks. It is well to start by feeding her in her new home. Then place a chair beside her, and sit down with a newspaper or a book for half an hour, talking to her from time to time, until she accepts the whole thing as normal procedure. A temperature of 60-65^{0}F., according to the season of the year, is desirable. Never have any kind of heating appliance on the floor or within reach of the bitch.Bitches are terribly restless both before and after birth, and an overturned heater could cause a disastrous fire. You may find that she is passing urine more frequently now and cannot last the night. So it is well to spread newspapers on the floor near her bed.

A bitch can have her litter in perfect safety any time after 59 to 60 days, although the ideal time is 63 days from mating, or 61 days from ovulation. So it is wise to make all arrangements well in advance, not forgetting to inform your veterinarian and ask him to be available if required. These gentlemen seem to have a habit of disappearing on a hunting or fishing trip at these times, and although German Shepherds are not normally difficult whelpers one should be prepared for any emergency, especially if it is a first litter for both bitch and owner.

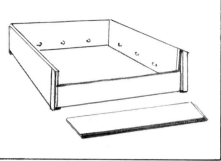

The whelping box.

PRUDENCE WALKER

Whelping Box

A strongly constructed wooden whelping box is essential. The cost will be saved several times over not only in time but in damage caused by the bitch seeking some suitable spot to give birth to her litter — on your silk cushions, on your own bed or chair, or even tearing up carpets and rugs to make a nest. The box will be a comfortable, safe place to house her babies when they are really fragile, during the first two or three weeks. It should be about four feet square with a removable front which can be slid in and out in slots. A depth of 15 inches is ideal. If the front is made in two parts (see Illustration) you can keep the very small puppies at home with the lower half and still make it easy for the mother, with her heavy "underneath," to get in and out without jumping. The upper half will be required when the puppies reach the exploratory age at about three weeks. We nail a metal (zinc) band all around the top edges as bitches are inclined to chew the wood in their labor. Inside, on the bottom, along the walls on each of the four sides, we screw in three heavy metal hooks with curved ends (cup hooks). These are not sharp nor can they be easily removed by the mother in her distress, and so do not constitute a danger. Over these hooks we stretch new burlap. This surface enables tiny claws to gain a footing without slipping on the wooden floor, and the puppies run no risk of stifling in loose blankets or bedding.

While the mother is in labor we keep thick newspaper under the burlap; these are easily slipped out and replaced with fresh ones to keep the bed clean and sweet during the birth of the puppies. The burlap is soaked in a pail of pine-scented disinfectant and water, rinsed and hung up to dry, and a fresh one put down two or three times each day. Burlap dries quickly. A point to remember is not to use any detergent powders for cleaning kennels or bedding; carbolic soap is better. We had a case recently where a valuable horse was lost;

the cause of death was found to be poison licked from the walls of its stall which were washed down with a strong detergent solution. There is evidently an ingredient in some of these powders that is poisonous to animals.

When the puppies are older and the mother leaves them alone for intervals, you will want some cozy bedding. We recommend wood shavings or "pine fiber"—the compressed wood shavings which can be teased up into a fluffy, soft bed that is well ventilated and can harbor no insects or sharp ends as does old-fashioned straw. Shredded newspaper is perfectly good too but it soon flattens down, particularly when damp, and it lacks the cozy quality of the pine fiber.

The mother will be able to rest away from them if they are warm and happily asleep in their own bed. She will not grow bored with her maternal duties if you start encouraging the puppies to be independent by making them comfortable once they begin to move around when their eyes open—at approximately two weeks. You will require a large, deep box or basket lined with a blanket in which to place the puppies while you clean out their whelping quarters. Moving them into the kitchen or a warm room where the mother can lie beside them will help her to accept this routine and not try to return them to the kennel by carrying them in her mouth. An infrared lamp of the kind used by pig or poultry breeders is of great help in very cold weather but it must be hung high so that the restless mother cannot knock it down.

Whelping

Having discussed housing let us now return to the well-being of the mother and the actual whelping. During her pregnancy she should be exercised normally, although towards the eighth week she may be too tired and heavy to walk far at one time. So give her two shorter outings since she must still be encouraged to move about as much as possible. Our breed is strong and courageous; normally the expectant mothers keep to their routine way of life right to the end. We had one who returned from a two mile walk without giving any signs of approaching her confinement, and went straight to her kennel and gave us her first-born within ten minutes.

In the whelping room we like to have a shelf somewhere out of dog reach (a flat basket suspended from the ceiling will do) in which to keep necessary equipment: absorbent cotton, antiseptic lotion, a pair of dull curved scissors, strong sewing silk, a rectal thermometer, a small flask of brandy, pieces of clean old linen, two small Turkish towels and a roll of sterile gauze. A hot water bottle enclosed in some soft woolen material like an old sweater is useful to place a cold puppy on. Surprisingly, a tiny puppy that appears lifeless will often revive if put in a warm place for a while, but it must be done immediately so have your hot water bottle already filled. Keep a notebook in which to note the time each puppy arrives, the sex and color (approximately — it will still be wet) and any details which may assist your vet if complications arise. These notes will be useful for future reference.

Now all is ready for the birth day. Your expectant mother will warn you that her time is near by making and remaking her bed, by showing a visible swelling of the vulva with discharge of mucus, and finally, with muscular contractions of the body. These begin gently like a sort of trembling, and increase more frequently and strongly with obvious spasms of sharp pain. The bitch will pant and perhaps cry a little between the contractions, and may be willing to drink a few spoonfuls of warm milk and water with syrup or honey added. You can usually expect the arrival of her first-born about an hour after the contractions commence but as we have already said, bitches vary considerably. The puppy will appear in a dark membranous bag containing fluid. If the delivery is easy, let the mother attend to everything herself. She has the know-how, and you need not worry even if she is usually a scatterbrain. We have often found that high spirited "naughty" females make the best brood bitches!

Should the puppy not be completely expelled following several contractions and strainings, take a firm but gentle hold of the bag with a small Turkish towel, and using gentle persuasion to coincide with the rhythm of her contractions pull down and under the belly towards her front, keeping a firm grip meanwhile. The puppy is normally presented head first; if so all should be quite easy for the mother. However a breech birth (hind feet first) may be more prolonged, and here your help with the towel and gentle downward pulls will help. Never jerk suddenly or upwards or you may cause a hemorrhage. In case the mother does not break the enveloping bag at once you must tear it open with your fingers, or the puppy will suffocate.

Once the umbilical cord is severed you can rub the whelp quite briskly with the towel to make it cry. The mother may be too exhausted to do this herself. However, if she is quiet, give her a few minutes to rest and recover, and she will then lick the puppy to encourage good circulation, bite through the cord, then devour the bag and afterbirth, or placenta.

The short interval is useful if you have to snip through the umbilical cord yourself, as the flow of blood from the cord to the placenta (or afterbirth) diminishes rapidly after delivery and there is less danger of severe bleeding. The cord is severed about an inch from the puppy's belly with dull scissors which crush the cord and prevent bleeding.

Destruction of the afterbirths, or most of them, is better for the mother. There are plenty of arguments that it is natural and right for her to devour them all, and an equal number that she should *not!* The first theory says that they help to cleanse the mother and "letdown" her milk supply; the second holds emphatically that the devouring of these rather nasty blood drenched membranes encourages cannibalism. We would rather take the middle course feeling that she should be allowed to eat two or three. We have found that if all are consumed it causes violent diarrhea, not in itself harmful, perhaps, but unpleasant and evil smelling in the kennel.

If a puppy appears lifeless do not give up hope. Rub it well with the Turkish towel, wipe out its mouth with gauze and swing it gently downwards a couple of times. If it still fails to wail, cover its mouth with yours and breathe in and out rhythmically — "the kiss of life" — and then wrap it up warmly on top of the hot water bottle.

The puppies should arrive at intervals of a few minutes to an hour between each delivery. If the delay is prolonged to more than three hours with hard straining on the part of the mother it is time to summon veterinary help. You should offer her small drinks between births and be generous with your praise and endearments. It is quite an ordeal for a bitch to give birth the first time and she will appreciate your concern and quiet presence, although we must add that occasionally one finds a brood bitch who wants to be left entirely alone and quite plainly says as much! In this case, put her in her whelping quarters with a large bowl of milk, water and honey, and apart from a brief look-in occasionally, leave her to her own devices. A bitch who shows an independent, even aggressive spirit at these times is usually not one to require help, but when something does go wrong, such bitches are usually sensible enough to allow themselves to be helped.

The German Shepherd puppy, except for the first few hours after birth, is really too large to be fed with an eyedropper. There are special pet nursing bottles available, or even a doll-sized bottle and nipple can be used when supplementary feeding is required.

XIII   Raising Puppies

When the litter is safely born (this may take 12-18 hours), have your veterinarian or an experienced breeder check that there are not dead puppies still inside the bitch. Put her on leash and coax her outside to relieve herself. You may be able to get her outside once or twice during the intervals between births. It helps if she will keep her bladder empty at this time and the walk, if only a few yards, will be good for her.

When she has been checked over, her hindquarters should be well sponged, being careful that the water is not too hot. Add a little of some disinfectant recommended for maternity cases and dry her thoroughly before putting her back with her babies who have in the meantime been kept warm in a basket or box.

Any dead or deformed puppies should be removed without the mother's knowledge. Just drop a towel over the poor pup and pick it up while she is busy with her other babies. On the fourth day, when you will have culled your litter (that is, decided how many and which puppies to retain if more than six or eight were delivered) examine the *hind* legs for dewclaws — the large claws which stick out like thumbs on the human hand — and have them removed. Your veterinarian will do this speedily and with very little pain. The mother will lick them and help the healing process, but she must be kept well out of hearing during the operation. Remember that it is only the *hind* dew claws which are removed in German Shepherds. Some litters, however, have no dewclaws at all, which saves a lot of trouble and indicates nothing except the effect of evolution on the dog; it is not a fault.

During birth there may be intervals of an hour or more when the busy mother can relax a little and even sleep for a few moments, although she will spend most of the time in licking the new babies to keep the circulation going and to encourage them to urinate. Try to tempt her with small drinks of warm milk. She may even eat one or two semi-sweet biscuits. Our own bitches seem pleased with a light snack during the long ordeal. And, to repeat, she must be persuaded to go outside to urinate when her delivery is completed; between the puppies' arrivals too, if she is willing.

For the first twelve hours she will require only a very light diet. You can beat up a couple of egg yolks and pour a cupful of boiling water over them, add a cupful of fresh milk and two tablespoons of evaporated milk with two crushed tablets of calcium with Vitamin D. Some jellied chicken broth (clear) is good. The next day, give a meal of boiled fresh fish carefully boned, adding a cupful of evaporated milk (diluted half and half) and the calcium as before.

If her food is deficient in calcium, she needs eight calcium tablets each day for the first week, and six during the remainder of the nursing period. This is not only excellent for replacing calcium in herself and supplying her puppies but it also helps to steady the flow of discharge from the uterus and generally assists in keeping mother and babies at their best.

The next meal should be her customary one of fresh meat or kibble. Then you can give a bowl of Cream of Wheat with milk at breakfast and keep your bitch on six meals per day for the first four or five weeks, gradually reducing the extras until she is having two meals of good meat and kibble, and a drink of milk night and morning, plus calcium (two tablets at each feed) until the puppies are weaned.

When the puppies are self-supporting you will have to reduce her food intake or she will put on weight that will be hard to take off. Stop all milk feeds and give her meat instead — three pounds in two meals with a little *dry* kibble mixed in or a few dry hard dog biscuits to crunch.

Start her on daily walks and give her a small dose (a teaspoonful is plenty) of ordinary Epsom salts for a day or two to help dry up the surplus milk. Some bitches like to visit their litter once or twice daily until the eighth week. Provided that the visit is only a brief one, we allow this as it seems to give comfort to the puppies and pleasure to their mother. A bitch usually enjoys having a family, and we feel that her happiness materially affects the puppies' character so we indulge her whims whenever possible.

When she is finally separated from the litter — particularly so if she is a show bitch — you may want to help restore her underline to normal. We use a large saucer half-filled with a mixture of rubbing alcohol and olive oil (half and half) gently dabbed onto the mammary glands with the fingers and repeated daily for four or five days. The alcohol dries up the milk and the oil keeps the skin soft and prevents painful cracking. If there are any tears in the tender skin smear them first with white Vaseline. A bath will help if conditions are right. Dry her well and keep her warm for a long time afterwards.

Weaning

At 12 to 14 days the puppies' eyes should open. If you feel that the mother is not attentive enough you can gently bathe the eyes with lukewarm boiled water to keep them free of mucus.

At two weeks they are ready to start eating meat, this being their most natural food. Take some lean beef and scrape it with a heavy

German Shepherds are excellent breeders, large litters being the rule rather than the exception. As we see here, they attend faithfully and diligently to their puppies' needs, regardless of disturbances and distractions.

sharp knife on a clean board, removing all sinews and skin. Put a tiny dab on the end of your finger and gently introduce it into the puppy's mouth. Some puppies will devour it at once and suck hard on your finger as if asking for more; others are slower and will "mouth" the pulp and may not take to it for the first few feeds. Do not give more than a scant teaspoonful the first two or three times. Feed once the first day and twice (morning and evening) on the six days following, gradually increasing the amount of meat pulp to a tablespoonful. Always put the babies back onto their mother's belly after each meat feed as this procedure helps them to digest.

There are on the market several brands of prepared puppy foods. On any one of these puppies will thrive after they are sixteen days old. Prepare the baby food according to package directions and feed it in a shallow dish at blood temperature (about 101°F.). Pour some of the gruel into the dish one eighth of an inch deep and let the puppies try to eat it. At each meal feed a little more, a little deeper layer in the

189

saucer. If you offer only milk, even no deeper than a quarter inch, the puppies will inhale it and be repelled. But if they can lap the gruel, they will be attracted to it and gradually learn not to dunk their noses.

Nailclipping

At the beginning of the fourth week each puppy should have its tiny white claw nails snipped carefully to prevent them from tearing the mother while nursing, and to encourage strong, well knuckled feet. Take great care to cut only the sharp tips, using really sharp curved scissors. If you have an accident and a toe is cut, dab on iodine at once. This operation should be repeated at ten day intervals until weaning is complete.

Early Handling

You must be prepared to give some time and plenty of patience to these progressive steps in the puppies' weaning. Personally I enjoy these close contacts with the little things best of all.

Puppies raised in a home will normally be handled regularly; however, it is just as important that puppies raised outdoors in a run

At six to seven weeks of age the puppy should be sound, sturdy and self-reliant. Notice that this one's ears are still down. As a general rule (but there are many exceptions), the larger the puppy the longer it takes for the ears to come up. In dog handler's parlance, this puppy, because of his large paws, would be said to have "good bone." Actually, the thickness is flesh and muscle. The knobby knees indicate that he will probably be a large dog. This is not a sign of Rickets.

or a kennel be picked up and handled daily. As we have seen elsewhere, the first few weeks of the dog's life are critical in his social relationships to people. In order that he should be well adjusted and learn to accept humans fully, he must be petted and handled at least once a day from the first or second week of his life until he goes into a new home. It is not enough to feed him and talk to him as you work about his quarters. There must be an actual physical contact made between dog and human.

A well-known doctor, going the rounds of a children's hospital ward, once wrote on the chart of a puny and backward infant, "This baby to be loved every two hours"; this is the keynote in puppy rearing. Puppies need fondling and care to develop the lovely companion-to-man nature of our breed and it greatly helps sturdy growth when they sense that they are in kind and understanding hands. Some may argue that this is unnatural. Our reply is that the little things are born under "unnatural" circumstances, and so they must be reared to take their place in our somewhat "unnatural" existence and will never be able to roam wild naturally.

Feeding the Growing Whelps

For those who wish to fuss rather than stick to commercial puppy food, here are my suggestions:

At the fifth week begin to feed cereal food; the best and easiest kind to give is wholewheat bread crumbs, crisped in a cool oven after baking. Pour hot milk over the crumbs in the proportion of ¼ pint to 2 large tablespoonsful of crumbs, add a little honey or Karo and leave to soak and swell a little. Introduce it in a shallow dish as I suggested earlier. The puppies may not eat very much but it is wise to get them accustomed to the taste and texture of various foods. From now on you can scald the crumbs (about a soup spoonful per puppy) with vegetable broth. Mix these moistened crumbs well into the pulped meat and feed twice daily, *gradually* increasing the quantities so that by the sixth week the puppies are eating as follows:

Two meals (10 a.m. and 4 p.m.) of one tablespoon (soaked in broth) crumbs or finely crushed wholewheat bread oven dried. Two tablespoons of pulped raw meat, 2 drops Halibut liver oil, ½ teaspoonful raw grated carrot (very fine) per puppy.

Two meals (7 a.m. and 10 p.m.) ¼ pint of Cream of Wheat (or semolina) with a little cold fresh milk, or two tablespoons of unsweetened evaporated milk, one crushed up calcium (with Vitamin D) tablet and one *small* teaspoonful of honey.

Take care that all food is only warm when fed; greedy puppies may gulp a few mouthfuls of very hot food and damage their tender mouths and throats. Separate them from the mother at least one hour before meal times so that they are really hungry and eager for food.

The changeover, however carefully made, to solid foods instead of mother's milk, may cause some looseness of the bowels; this is only temporary as a rule. If it persists, give a half teaspoonful of milk of magnesia to each puppy to correct the acidity. By this time the babies will be nearly self supporting and the mother will be weary of them and want to regain her own strength, so if she nurses them three or four times each day (especially early morning and late evening) she will be doing her duty nicely. She must be able to get away from the litter at will and this can be achieved either by a *large* " cat-door" like those fixed on house doors so that cats can roam at will, or by a bench in the whelping kennel onto which she can jump when she wants her rest untormented by the babies. With the cat door arrangement she must have a porch or enclosure to which she can go to escape the cold or rain.

Worming

When your puppies are a full six weeks old give them their first and all important dosing for Roundworms. These are present in all puppies to a greater or less degree, and do not reflect discredit on the breeder! It is wise to consult your veterinarian about the correct vermifuge. Take the average weight of the puppies by weighing two or three and ask for the dose giving weight, age, and breed.

The vet will probably supply piperazine for Roundworms. You will be instructed to mix it with the puppies' food. We like to give the vermifuge in the early morning. Repeat the dose ten or eleven days later because while you destroy the worms in the intestines with the first dose, you do not kill the larvae in the blood. So you must wait until the larvae have become worms and kill them with this second dose. It is impossible for a puppy to thrive with these parasites sapping the nourishment it so urgently requires at this juncture, so deworming should be carried out with scrupulous care.

Recently a drug has been offered by veterinarians which destroys Roundworms, Whipworms and Hookworms. In the United States it is called Task. Your dog's doctor may supply you with it if he finds from a fecal examination that the puppies have Hookworm as well.

Seventh Week

Entering their seventh week, your puppies should be almost completely weaned, and you must increase all foods gradually over the following week so that their digestion is not overtaxed or their stomachs distended. By now, the mother will most probably have finished with them, although we like to allow her a short visit at bedtime for a few days longer if she is interested. There is no prettier picture than a mother playing with her sturdy active family. We consider these sentimental moments our reward for the long hours of work attached to the successful rearing of a litter.

You can ease the first few days of weaning (when the puppies suffer more from thirst than hunger as they are not yet accustomed to drinking much water) by giving a bowlful of milk and warm water at 2 p.m. and 7 p.m. between the other meals. It need not be continued as their stomachs soon expand to take enough food for several hours at a time.

Eighth Week

Increase food quantities, especially the meat, gradually. Watch carefully for any greedy feeders; these must be held back while slow or backward ones are put to the bowl first or fed separately.   By the ninth week the meat for each puppy should be 12-16 ounces per day (divided between two meals) and as much bread or kibble as it will readily eat, six drops Halibut liver oil (or one teaspoonful olive oil and ½ teaspoonful seaweed powder), one soup spoonful of finely grated raw carrot, a little hot broth poured over and well mixed up.

For breakfast at 7:30 a.m., each puppy will require a level tablespoon of semolina or Cream of Wheat sprinkled into ½ pint water and boiled for ten minutes. Sweeten with a large teaspoonful of honey or lard adding two crushed tablets of calcium with Vitamin D.

This meal is repeated at 10:30 p.m. and you can save time and trouble by making sufficient porridge in the morning, adding the other ingredients at feeding time. Similarly the whole day's supply of meat can be ground at once and kept in a cool place until required. If refrigerated, it must be brought up to room temperature before feeding or colic or diarrhea may be the unhappy result.

Avoid an excess of fat in their meat, and feed all meals warm for easier digestion. Never leave any food in the kennel or pen. If it is not eaten in a reasonable period of time, remove it and throw it out, feeding less at the next meal until all is eaten every time. Puppies' appetites are similar to our own and vary a little at times without any special cause, although constant refusal to eat should be investigated.

Give only large shin or marrow bones so that no splinters can be gnawed off to damage tender mouths. These bones should always have been boiled in their broth or baked in the oven; if fed raw they can easily become maggoty from flies, and this causes diarrhea. Bones are very helpful when teething, and for forming strong jaws; if fed at night or after meals they encourage the gastric juices and aid digestion. Do not give excessive vitamins and pills in an effort to produce super puppies. Overdosing of vitamins is extremely dangerous and calcium abcesses are caused by too generous doses.

Avoid irregular feeding. We have timed the early and late meals with half an hour's difference during the weaning period (that is 7 a.m. instead of 7:30 a.m.)as the very small puppy cannot adjust itself at once to the long night without warmth or nursing from the mother.

Commercial Diets

I have already said, " If you want to fuss." There is nothing wrong with fussing if you enjoy it. The above instructions have been included because I know that thousands of dog breeders do feed this way, not only from tradition but because they like to feel that the dog or dogs are part of the family so they feed them like humans, and by preparing their food personally feel fulfilled.

Some of the top nutrition authorities who work with dogs in large numbers, tell us that it is unnecessary to prepare individual meals. They find that puppies can be raised even more rapidly and soundly by feeding them — starting long before weaning — a thoroughly tested prepared dog food and nothing else but water. If you do not have the time to spend preparing the meals we have included, don't feel guilty. Instead, consider using one of these complete diets.

If you are still not convinced, I suggest that you divide a litter in two. Feed half of it your way, or the way we have described above; feed the other half on a nutritionally balanced prepared dog food. Old timers who have spent years working out formulas and mixing ingredients have been amazed to find that puppies fed in the simplest possible manner do just as well, and frequently better, than those receiving home prepared diets.

Sanitation

The bedding and sawdust, or newspapers, on which the puppies relieve themselves must be changed frequently — bedding twice daily, and sawdust four to six times according to the season and whether or not they can be allowed outdoors.

Pesticides

If you must use insect powder or spray during these early weeks, cover the puppy's eyes and nose with a piece of gauze during the application; these organs are highly sensitive to pesticides.

No Visitors

Keep all visitors away from the litter for the first week and do not allow young children to handle the puppies. A small delicate leg can be broken or dislocated by unskilled hands, or a heavy puppy can easily be dropped and have its head or back damaged permanently.

Outdoor Exercise

We put the puppies outside in a box in a sheltered sunny place for a few minutes each day when they are between three and four weeks old, then increase the periods gradually until they are running about and can get into their sheltered bed or box (protected from strong sun or rain) by themselves. They must never be allowed to lie down to sleep on concrete or cold damp earth. Nor should puppies ever be left in strong sunlight without cover. German Shepherds do not usually like the hot sun or bright light, so make sure a shady area is accessible in their exercise area.

Water

It is better to offer a drink of fresh water each time you visit the litter and after the main meals; if water is left with the puppies they will play in it and soil it, making it undrinkable.

Maturity and Growth

It is as well to remember that we are dealing with a slowly maturing breed but one that grows from an average 16 ounces at birth to anywhere from 65 to 80 pounds when one year old!

Maturity and growth must therefore not be confused; the former is the perfection of the latter and comes about slowly in the German Shepherd which goes through a "knees and elbows" stage like any teenager! If maturity is slow then it is compensated for by the lasting quality of our breed. We frequently see youthful ten and even twelve year old dogs enjoying life to the full because they were kept in hard condition on a correct diet. It is sheer self indulgence on the owner's part to feed tidbits and candies to their pets. A small cube of plain cheese or boiled liver is just as tasty and is, as well, beneficial.

It is not unusual for a puppy's knees to be "knobby" and this is sometimes mistaken by the uninitiated for rickets. This is very far from the truth. It is much more likely to indicate that the puppy will be a large dog. Puppies raised on the diets we have indicated are hardly likely to be suffering from that deficiency disease which is characterized by soft, easily bent or broken bones.

Maturity comes slowly in the German Shepherd, which goes through a "knees and elbows" stage like any teenager!

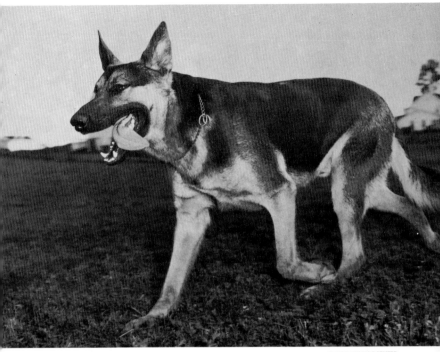

This is the famous German Shepherd stride. The diagonally opposite front and rear legs move together, thus imparting a fluidity of movement unmatched by any other dog.

XIV   The Stud Dog and His Mating

This chapter is of more concern to the serious breeder, but if a dog has a particularly good pedigree or has won success in the show ring it might encourage his owner to offer the dog's service at stud. But before attempting it any prospective breeder should witness some stud services, and if he is allowed to assist in a German Shepherd mating so much the better.

Except for a widely campaigned and advertised dog with a great show record, stud work is not nearly so rewarding as many people imagine.

Since the German Shepherd is a slowly maturing dog, he is not normally ready for stud service until well into his second year. He might be tried at 15 or 16 months to prove his ability (and fertility) but he ought not to be used regularly until after he is 18 months old.

Try to find an experienced and willing matron for his first service — the attitude of his initial mate can make or mar his stud career. It is quite usual to offer a free service to the first bitch served, with a puppy as payment if the union is successful.

You should not exercise the dog before the mating. In our experience, the owner of the visiting bitch is invariably late and quite often the bitch is uncooperative so that much time can be wasted in effecting a union, so be prepared to give up the day if your dog is expecting a visit. Many troubles are caused by the bitches being brought before their time, or after. We have suggested some tests to determine the readiness of the bitch in Chapter VII and you to determine the readiness of the bitch in Chapter XII and you not experienced. It is wise too, to tactfully suggest that the bitch be properly exercised beforehand so that she arrives empty and comfortable after her journey. Neither animal should be fed before the event, or allowed to drink much water.

Select a quiet place where there are as few distractions as possible and where the two dogs can play together for their courting — if the bitch is ready and willing. Do not be alarmed if the stud nibbles her ears or neck, plays leapfrog or rushes round her like crazy. This is all to the good as long as he does not exhaust himself. Note his behavior so that you will know what to expect on future occasions. A dog almost always goes to work in the same manner, and a handler who knows the dog can be a great help.

We like to put down a wide strip of coconut matting for the pair to stand on. Then the dog's hind feet do not slip when he mounts; it is also useful in keeping the bitch steady.

Ask the owner (or helper) to hold the bitch firmly at each side of the neck, ready to grasp her head between the knees if necessary to keep her from struggling or snapping and turning on the dog when he tries to penetrate. You should be on her right side with an arm underneath to prevent her dropping her rear end at the wrong moment, a maneuver bitches seem to be expert in right from the start.

If the act is not accomplished after a few attempts, do not allow the dog to exhaust himself; take him outside on the leash or put him in his kennel for a few minutes rest while the bitch calms down. If she is very bad-tempered she can be muzzled in the manner shown in our chapter on First Aid. Talk to the dog soothingly and see that the visitor's owner keeps calm too!

We do not want to suggest that all matings are difficult. Many are completed easily and smoothly, and cause no concern, but the stud owner should know what to do when there is trouble. When dealing with a maiden it is well to smear in and around her genital parts white Vaseline on a sheathed finger tip. (You will find a list of required equipment for the mating at the end of this Chapter.) If the dog has the misfortune to ejaculate without entering and the penis enlarges outside of the bitch's body, let him mount the bitch and make his sexual motions and the penis will quickly shrink. If you try holding him away from the bitch it may not go down for a long while.

Let us assume that both dogs are cooperative and have had a brief period of courtship. The bitch's owner will be in control of her head while you will hold her rear up with the hind legs well parted, and encourage your dog to mount. When he does, try not to interfere as he clasps his mate with his front feet around her waist. Hold her with your arm as far back as possible underneath and keep her tail well to one side. After entry is effected, hold the dog on the bitch's back for a minute or two, then allow him to turn naturally. Some dogs turn one way, some another, and you should note this the first time. Help him if he is in difficulty by guiding his hind leg gently over the bitch's back so that he turns completely and stands back to back to his mate and both pulling in opposite directions, still tied in position by his swelling inside her vagina. He will stay tied there by muscular contraction of his own aided by contractions of the bitch until the ejaculation of semen is completed. This can continue from a few minutes to an hour, although the usual period is 25 to 35 minutes. Don't handle the dogs while they are tied. Too much handling shortens the period of tying. When the dog withdraws, do not let the bitch run around excitedly. Quickly return her to her kennel or the car, and let her rest without water to drink for at least half an hour.

The dog, too, should be returned to his sleeping quarters. If the mating has been difficult or prolonged, give him egg yolk beaten up in milk, or some honey or Karo dissolved in tepid milk. Let him rest well before giving him his usual walk. Occasionally, the owner of the bitch asks for a double service, particularly if the bitch is either a maiden or an older matron who would be too old for service at a future heat. This should be allowed if it does not interfere with the dog's other commitments.

Remember that one good litter is a much better recommendation for the stud than two services without issue, so use all your patience and restraint to help your dog and his visitor to obtain satisfaction all around. A veterinarian's help may have to be sought if a refractory bitch does not respond to her owner's efforts or the advances of the stud dog. In such a case a mild sedative can be given or, by exploration of the organs, the doctor may discover an abnormality.

There is no blame attached to the dog that attempts a mating and fails. So many factors govern the mating: the correct date, the journey, the environment, whether either animal has been fed too near the event, or insufficiently exercised beforehand, just to name a few. And we add to this the not infrequent reason of the over-pampered pet so spoiled that it will not allow itself to be handled by anyone not of the sex of its owner, or worse-not to be handled at all!

As we mentioned earlier, stud work is only for the experienced or those prepared to obtain experience, and the rewards are not nearly so great as popularly supposed. It is never worthwhile, unless you live in very remote territory, to keep a stud dog just to service your own bitches. You can hire the best stud in the country cheaper than you can keep a dog in your kennel who must be well fed and housed, and who will cause complications if your bitches are in heat and his services are not required.

The fee for a stud service should be agreed on beforehand. It can be either a " choice of litter" or a monetary fee. If the latter, it is usual to pay at the time of service. If the fee is to be a puppy, then there should be a clear understanding as to the age at which the puppy is to be selected and taken. Agreement should be entered into beforehand as to whether there is to be a free return service if the first fails to take.

Here is a list of the things to have on hand for the mating:

Small tube (not a breakable jar) of white Vaseline.

Thin surgical rubber finger sheath.

Gauze bandage for muzzling.

Clean linen for dog if a sling is required after precipitate ejaculation.

Paper towels or tissues.

A pair of loose fitting thick gloves to handle an " offish" visitor.

Low stool (we use an oldfashioned milking stool) to sit on during the period of the " tie".

An inexhaustible supply of patience.

Proper feeding and ample exercise are the fundamentals required for good health.

XV   Health

There is no substitute for a good and trusted veterinarian when illness or accident endangers your dog, but if you watch his general health and know how to deal with minor ailments, you will not need to call for professional help too frequently.

It is a great help to be able to take your dog's temperature correctly and to record it so that your vet can be informed if he asks. A dog's normal temperature is 101.2°F. A young puppy can have a reading of up to 102.2°F. without being sick. Keep a rectal thermometer ready for use in your first aid box. Grease it with white Vaseline and insert it gently into the rectum preferably with the dog lying on his side. Make sure you keep it there long enough to make a true recording.

Constipation

One of the common causes of illness in dogs is Constipation. The cause may be wrong feeding by indulgent owners who are so "kind" to their pets that they feed them on human foods containing sugar, spices, refined flour, and other ingredients which block the canine intestine and ruin the dog's appetite, and cause him to reject his correct diet.

An old and very experienced cattleman of our acquaintance used to say that true success with animals lay in the eye of the master,

An old and very experienced breeder used to say that true success with animals lay in "the eye of the master," meaning that a close watch had to be kept on all details by the person in charge. When a dog is alert, clear-eyed, glossy-coated, clean-eared, and walks with a swagger, it indicates that he is feeling well.

meaning that a close watch had to be kept on all details by the person in charge. And so it is with your dog who cannot say that he feels unwell in so many words, but can give you distress signals in several ways; it is up to you to learn to recognize them.

Note the state of his daily eliminations every day. The feces should be brown in color and passed without straining; clay color denotes a liver disturbance, and black or dark feces could mean a bowel hemorrhage. This last is one of the occasions when you will need veterinary advice.

For a liver disturbance, if the dog is not badly distressed, make sure he is not chilled from sleeping on a cold floor. Take him off all fats, oils and cow milk, and feed fresh raw meat with finely grated carrot incorporated with parsley and watercress too, if he will take them. You may have to give ground meat for a day or two so that the vegetables can be mixed with the meat; if the dog is hungry he will eat without noticing the additions. Stop bread or kibble for a day or two and give evaporated milk diluted with water and a little natural honey added. Increase his daily exercise to stimulate his functions and give a tablespoonful of milk of magnesia early in the morning for two or three days or until he is normal again.

If the feces are hard-packed or dry and crumbly in consistency, dose with a tablespoon of mineral oil and mix a soupspoon of pure olive oil into his main meal. If the dog strains and cannot pass feces, he may have a slight stoppage caused by bone fragments, or from eating garbage, in which case he should be given an enema — a pint of lukewarm water with a tablespoonful of olive oil added. This must be administered with the utmost care to avoid giving pain to the sufferer. Let the fluid flow into the rectum very slowly with frequent pauses, and have plenty of newspapers handy as results can be instant.

A day's fast on honey and water can work wonders in simple cases of Constipation or digestive disturbances caused by overeating or from unsuitable foods. By completely resting the system, the dog can soon recover. Do not worry if he goes even 48 hours without solid foods, so long as he has plenty of liquids such as milk, water and honey, and clear beef or chicken broth.

Diarrhea

Diarrhea is another sure sign that all is not well with your dog. In puppies it can be the result of simple teething trouble. A teaspoonful of milk of magnesia with a half day's fast on liquids as mentioned above will rest the system. Usually the trouble subsides in 24 hours if there is no high temperature. After the fast give a bowl of cornstarch prepared as follows: moisten two tablespoons of cornstarch with cold water in a thick bowl, then stir in boiling water until the mixture is thick and clear like the old fashioned dress starch. Add two large tablespoons of white sugar and some evaporated milk; cool well before feeding. This is an excellent remedy for a simple case of diarrhea or upset stomach and can be repeated until relief is obtained.

Coughing

Coughing is another of your pet's signals to show that all is not well. In itself a cough is not a lone symptom; it indicates a condition which must be diagnosed before treatment. First of all, examine his throat, opening the mouth wide and shining a flashlight in. Explore carefully with the forefinger to see if there is a bone, a fragment of wood or some other article that may have been picked up and swallowed. The removal of any sharp article embedded in the tender membranes of the throat or mouth is a job for your veterinary surgeon, but a fish bone can sometimes be sent down the gullet by force feeding a piece of soft bread about half the size of an egg. Massage the front of the throat and neck gently and thoroughly to encourage swallowing.

A healthy dog is always ready for a romp. When he lies around, is listless and begins to just pick at his food, best check for the cause.

The old-fashioned pneumonia jacket can give speedy relief and often prevent a long illness.

Bronchitis

Labored breathing along with a cough usually means some kind of Bronchitis, or even Pneumonia or Distemper; if so, you will want professional advice at once. Some dogs persist in hanging their heads out of the car window and the dust and fumes give them a sore throat and slight cough. This can be relieved by a syrup mixture of honey, glycerine and lemon juice in equal proportions. This old remedy is very soothing if a small teaspoonful is placed on the back of the tongue at hourly intervals until the cough subsides. When the dog has had a chill due to exposure, a little camphorated oil smeared onto the chest and the wearing of the old fashioned "pneumonia jacket" can give speedy relief and often prevents a long illness. (See the illustration above.)

To make the jacket take a piece of thin blanket or heavy woolen material, oblong in shape, and long enough to cover the dog from chest to loins. Cut it somewhat narrower at the chest end, and stitch this narrow end down with strong oversewing in a hem wide enough to allow a strong tape to be drawn through. Draw this up and fasten it collarwise around the dog's neck. It will be bunched up, but loose and comfortable. Stitch two more tapes, one on each side behind the shoulders, and another two, one on each side above the loins. The aim is to keep the chest and brisket covered until the dog recovers. One advantage of this homemade jacket is that small strips can be snipped off with scissors so that the patient is gradually " returned to normal" without suddenly feeling the loss of his extra covering.

Rest and warmth are always recommended when a dog is sick. By warmth we do not mean artificial warmth unless the weather is very cold, but a snug bed away from cold winds and off the floor. If the room is large or the ceiling high, a blanket can be hung over the bed as a canopy. If heavy chairs are placed at each side of the bed and two cords stretched across, the blanket can be slung over them; this will keep the dog's natural body heat in the bed. We have found this better than putting the dog close to any kind of heating appliance or fire, as direct heat seems to make him restless and he will move out into some cool spot, exactly the reverse of what he requires.

Anal Glands

The purpose of these two glands, one on each side at the base of the anus, is not known. They secrete a yellowing fluid which sometimes hardens, causing the dog to scoot his rectum across the floor in an attempt to relieve the discomfort. Place a layer of cotton or a wad of tissue over the hand and lay it across the anus. Squeeze with the thumb and middle finger behind and slightly below the glands which will feel like small lumps inside the skin, forcing their contents onto the protective cotton which should then be burned.

Convulsions

Teething fits sometimes occur in young puppies, or when they are under strain from the rapid pace of growth. In all cases the sufferer should be removed to a small darkened kennel or room where there are no pieces of furniture which can be knocked over and injure him should the attack return. You may cover his head with a towel or blanket to quiet him enough to move him but give him air again as soon as possible. Most occasional fits are traced either to a dietary deficiency, to worms or to overexposure to unaccustomed hot sun.

A general rule of thumb is that when a puppy loses awareness of his surroundings during a convulsion it is due to brain damage (encephalitis) caused by a virus; however, if he retains awareness it may be due to a toxin which might be from food or worms. The outlook for an uncomplicated recovery from the latter is good provided the cause is determined and the trouble corrected. Unfortunately, virus induced fits frequently leave a dog with nerve damage which might manifest itself as twitches (Chorea). Sometimes these disappear or diminish as the dog matures, but there is no way of foretelling.

A bland diet to rest the digestive system is recommended. Cream of wheat and honey, egg yolks and milk, cottage cheese and some well boiled tripe in milk are suitable foods. Absolute quiet is essential and your veterinarian will probably prescribe bromide in suitable dosage. Quantity varies according to age and condition so we cannot suggest it here.

Nursing bitches sometimes suffer from convulsions known as Eclampsia. These are caused by the calcium drain on the system when carrying or suckling a large litter. When this happens, remove the puppies at once to a warm place and feed them evaporated milk and water with a medicine dropper. This will keep them contented until a foster mother can be found, or the dam recovers. You may help her by giving her three or four calcium and vitamin D tablets crushed up finely in milk and honey but if your vet can give her an intravenous injection of calcium at the earliest opportunity it will put her right.

Teething fits in puppies can usually be handled with small doses of milk of magnesia (one teaspoonful) each morning for three or four days. It is wise to check for worms as they are notoriously hard to get rid of in some dogs, and you may have just an obstinate case on your hands even after dosing. See that the puppy has a good supply of large hard bones to chew on at this time. Gnawing promotes gastric juices and it soothes his nerves to have an occupation when he has toothache.

Vomiting

Vomiting has a number of causes; many of them are not really serious. If he is a country dog he may merely have been eating grass or green oats. Sometimes drinking very cold water after heavy exercise or excitement will cause vomiting, particularly if he romps soon after eating.

Worms in the stomach is another cause; he may even throw up worms, but the puppy should recover quickly when these have been eliminated by proper dosing. (See the chapter on Parasites.)

If the dog is excessively thirsty and vomits mucus and water after drinking he probably is having a gastric or gastroenteritis attack and will require professional advice.

Distemper and Infectious Hepatitis

These two are known as the "killer" diseases. Distemper (correctly called Carre's Disease after the man who studied it) affects the central nervous system and hepatitis affects the liver. Unfortunately, there are no known cures for either of these viral infections so the symptoms have to be treated as they occur. Both Distemper and Hepatitis can be prevented by proper immunization and no one who truly loves dogs will keep one that has not been inoculated. Symptoms, at the beginning, are much the same. There is usually a fever, a discharge from eyes and nose, and sometimes vomiting. The most obvious sign is a rocketing temperature. Diarrhea is common, and Pneumonia can be an added complication. The dog seems to recover for a time, but worse then follows. Fits and frequently death ensue. Twitching of the limbs, called Chorea, is often a complication of Distemper from which the dog may suffer for the rest of its life.

If a mature dog lives through the first two days of Hepatitis, he usually recovers. Frequently one or even both eyes may turn milk glass blue after an attack of Hepatitis. This is not serious and it will disappear within a few days.

As these diseases are highly contagious, keep all other dogs out of range of the sick one, and change your clothing, especially shoes and stockings, if you must go near other dogs.

Leptospirosis

Also known as Infectious Jaundice, there are two types of Leptospirosis — *Canicola* and *Icterohaemorrhagiae*. These diseases to the uninitiated are similar in appearance to Distemper. The incubation period is five to fifteen days. Weakness, loss of appetite, vomiting and a temperature of $103°$ to $105°$ are often symptoms of Leptospirosis. At the onset, the dog suffers a sharp drop in temperature, becomes quite depressed, breathes laboriously, and evinces a great thirst. This thirst is seldom present in attacks of Distemper. The dog also seems stiff and sore, particularly when rising from a sitting position.

Leptospirosis is a disease spread by rats. It is often contracted from drinking water which has been contaminated by the urine of rats as well as from garbage dumps where rats have lived. This is why cleanliness and sanitation are so important in the care of your dog.

Any of the above mentioned symptoms are warnings to contact your veterinarian. While there is some mortality with Leptospirosis, antibiotic treatment in the early stages can reduce the danger considerably. Your veterinarian will know what to do.

Tracheobronchitis

Usually called "Kennel Cough" this is a common ailment of puppies. It is characterized by a dry gagging cough which is usually more severe at night. In every other respect the puppy appears okay; even his temperature is normal. Fortunately, Kennel Cough is a self-limiting disease; this means that the dog usually recovers without treatment, although coughing may continue for as long as for six weeks. There are dog cough syrups available to ease his raw throat, or a child's cough syrup may be used. For severe cases your vet may prescribe one of the antibiotic drugs which frequently relieve the problem.

Convalescence

Convalescence from these diseases is long; it requires much skill and care to restore the constitution that is so much a part of this breed. Care must be exercised in not allowing the dog to overtire himself in the joy of feeling better. Prolonged romping with another and stronger dog is particularly exhausting, so keep his boisterous playmates' visits brief.

Egg yolks (these can be scrambled with butter for a change and some dried whole wheat bread crumbled into the custard) may be fed with cow milk, or if at all possible, goat milk, with plenty of nature's own chosen restorative, natural honey. An old hen well boiled with carrots, onions and garlic and the flesh carefully boned and chopped with bread is also tasty and helps the dog's appetite. If the resulting stock is reduced by rapid boiling and put under refrigeration when cool, it will "jell" and make an excellent snack for the convalescent animal. It is also helpful to bring down a high temperature, as a feverish dog will usually lick anything cold.

Beef jelly is also very good and can be made by placing gravy beef (shin beef) in cold water and leaving it in a covered pan in a low heated oven overnight. Strain, add one or two envelopes of powdered gelatine, cool and refrigerate. Do not add salt or seasoning to these preparations. A dog with a high fever will sometimes lick ice cream. Buy the best brand of plain vanilla or better still make some from egg yolks and fresh cream flavored with honey. This can be a life saver for a dangerously sick dog.

Hip problems are less likely to develop in dogs that are exercised regularly.

Hip Dysplasia

There has been a great deal of discussion regarding Hip Dysplasia, or as it is sometimes called, subluxation, particularly as related to the German Shepherd. For some reason which is as yet unknown, but probably due to the popularity of the German Shepherd, this problem seems to be associated in the minds of the public with this one breed. Let us begin by saying that it is not true. Subluxation is found in many breeds of dogs although it seems limited primarily to the larger ones. It may also surprise the reader to learn that subluxation is present in many other animals, other than the dog and is also a problem with humans.

Hip Dysplasia or subluxation — are they the same thing and how can they be recognized?

For our purposes, we can consider Hip Dysplasia and subluxation as being the same, although there is a technical distinction, subluxation being considered the precursor to Dysplasia.

In any event, what we are concerned with are the hip problems. The upper end of the hind leg bone (the femur) normally fits into a socket (acetabulum) in the bony girdle or pelvis. The hind legs are held in place by large, bunchy muscles. Any one who has felt the thighs of a racing Greyhound will know what I am talking about. When the socket is not fully formed, or if the femur does not fit in properly or is not held in place tightly by the muscles, hip problems develop. These can range from one so mild that it is noticeable only on X-ray to such a severe case that the dog is incapacitated. Usually, clinical symptoms appear anywhere between the ages of four months to two years. These can be manifested as an unsteadiness in the dog's gait, pain when arising, difficulty in climbing stairs, inability of reluctance to jump, etc.

In spite of all the studies made, we are as yet uncertain as to the actual cause of Hip Dysplasia. In the human, this condition can be diagnosed at birth. In the dog, even severe cases cannot be diagnosed before he is two weeks old and usually not before he is three to four months of age. This refers to both clinical and X-ray diagnosis. While some investigators have ascribed a hormonal basis for Hip Dysplasia, it is no more predominant in one sex than the other. The only reason at the present time for the belief in a hormonal basis is that under laboratory conditions the administration of certain hormones has caused subluxation.

Heredity is certainly the biggest single factor involved in the condition. However, those who *ipso facto* state " subluxation is always caused by an inherited factor" have no scientific support for that statement. As we said, heredity plays its role in the condition; however, statistically, all that can be said is that about half the total variation is caused by genetic factors. The other fifty percent is accounted for by environmental factors.

We have been talking up until now about all grades of severity. Because of the wide variance in subluxation however, it has been divided into four grades. Grade One, which is the mildest form, probably would not affect the dog's function as a pet; Grade Two would be noticeable, but it is probable that the dog could still play a happy role as a family pet, Grades Three and Four are so serious as to probably incapacitate the dog. In one study, 5,072 German Shepherds were X-rayed. Of these, the X-rays of 2,247 or 44% showed some sign of Hip Dysplasia. However, many of these dogs (we do not have the exact number) were capable of leading normal lives. In fact, it is probable that their Dysplasia would not even have been suspected if they had not been routinely X-rayed. The odds against its being of a crippling or incapacitating nature are substantial.

One thing which can be done, and should be done, is to avoid having your puppy excessively fat. Particularly in the early stages, while the muscles are developing, there is reason to believe that too much weight puts a strain on the dog which would dispose him towards this problem. Excercise which would tend to develop the muscles and at the same time reduce the body fat is also indicated.

Nor should the hereditary factor be ignored. Make every effort to secure your puppy from stock which is as free as possible of the factor. An interesting sidelight is that while Hip Dysplasia is almost unknown in working Greyhounds, one study made in Finland where Greyhounds are kept primarily as pets, showed that a number of the dogs had subluxation. An indication that great size is a factor would be that one study showed that such giant dogs as St. Bernards and Newfoundlands had an 82% and 64% incidence respectively.

So you can see that to equate the German Shepherd with this problem is not only unfair, but untrue. Perhaps it is as well though that the German Shepherd breeders are aware of this problem, because a very great and conscientious effort is being made to overcome this defect by breeding only from sound dogs.

What can you do should your dog develop subluxation? The first thing you should do is to consult your veterinarian who will undoubtedly X-ray the dog to verify the condition. There are a number of things which can relieve the problem, such as certain steroids (available only on prescription) which will alleviate the pain and allow the dog to exercise more normally. You can watch his weight, follow your veterinarian's advice, and there is a fair, if not a good chance, that while your dog may never pull a sled or leap nine foot fences he will lead a relatively normal life and live to a ripe age.

Picking up objects that have been contaminated by other animals can be a source of parasitic infection.

XVI   Parasites

Worms

Worms are prevalent among dogs, particularly when they are puppies. Some estimates of the incidence run as high as 90%

infection at sometime during their life. That is, 90 % of all the dogs you see or own are likely to have worms at one time or another. This is not as serious as it may sound since many dogs seem to live with the worms, suffering little, if any, ill effects from their infestation. However, a dog should never be allowed to harbor worms. Your veterinarian has the means for diagnosing their presence, differentiating between the types, and medicating your dog relatively safely and simply in order to remove them.

It is usually necessary to take a stool specimen to your veterinarian. Only a small amount is required, approximately a thimbleful and this should be taken in a glass jar labeled with your name and the name of your dog. The veterinarian will separate the eggs from the feces and make a microscopic examination.

Some general symptoms which should cause one to suspect worm infestation are as follows: A bloated stomach — particularly when infested with Roundworms, a puppy's stomach will blow up out of all proportion to his body. Some types of worms cause extreme emaciation. The dog has a normal appetite but does not seem to put on weight. A cough which lasts for only a few days may be due to the presence of worm eggs in the esophagus. Watery eyes and/or runny nose are also worm symptoms.

Heavy mucus of the nose and/or eyes, however, is usually a symptom of a more serious ailment requiring immediate veterinarary attention. Frequently a dog will sit on his haunches and drag his rear end along the ground. This is commonly mistaken a symptom of worms. It is usually due, however, to impacted anal glands, a subject which we dicussed on page 206. If you do not feel able to express these glands yourself, the vet will have to do it for you.

How Dogs Contract Worms

Most worm infections come from worm eggs passed in the stool. When a dog sniffs around where other dogs have defecated, he picks them up on his nose, licks it, swallows them, and is infected. Sometimes an owner will carry worm eggs home on his shoes. A nursing puppy may be infected by his mother or from feces on her feet. Hookworms can even enter through the dog's skin, particularly if he is kept in filthy surroundings. Tapeworms are carried by fleas which serve as intermediary host, and when a dog nips at and swallows a flea, he swallows the Tapeworm as well.

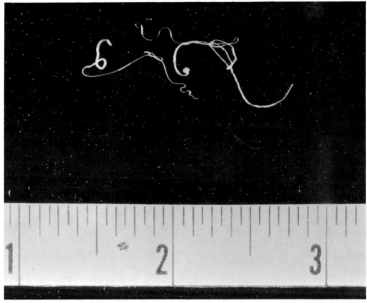

Whipworms!

Whipworms

Whipworms are more common in the south and other warmer areas of the country. They are seldom if ever encountered in very young puppies, being primarily an ailment of dogs three months of age or older. Whipworm eggs incubate in the soil for about six weeks during warm weather. However, the eggs are highly resistant to freezing and may be dormant for years until the warming of the soil enables them to maturate. The worm remains in the eggs and lies dormant until swallowed. The dog's digestive juices dissolve the egg's coating, liberating the parasite which then attaches itself to the dog's intestine. The Whipworm is not as common as the other three, and it too can be eliminated by proper medication.

Roundworms

Roundworms are more dangerous to the puppy than to the older dog which seems to develop a kind of resistance to them. However, they

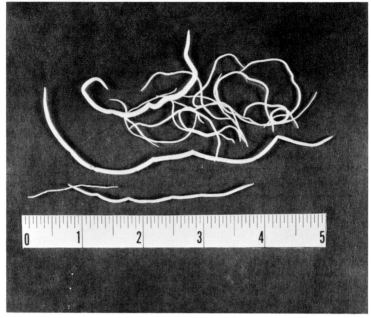

PURINA PET CARE CENTER

Roundworms!

have been known to cause death to puppies. This is the worm most often seen by the dog owner. The adult worm is long and spaghetti-like in appearance and when expelled by the dog, either by vomiting or in the stool, the worms coil themselves into a characteristic watch spring shape; hence, the name " Roundworm."

Roundworm larvae can infect the bloodstream of a pregnant bitch and through her be passed on to the puppy. This is why it is so important to worm a pregnant mother in the early stages of gestation. However, should this be overlooked, it is best to worm the puppies when they are two or three weeks old and again when they are four to five weeks old. A medication based on a drug called piperazine can be given, either directly in a capsule or pill, or as a powder in the food or drink. This treatment should be repeated in twelve or thirteen days in order to destroy any newly hatched worms which were still in the egg at the first dosing. The trick is to give the eggs time to hatch and then eliminate the worms before they, in their turn, have had time to get old enough to lay eggs.

Hookworms

These are tiny parasites the size of a thread and only a half inch long in contrast to the Roundworm which can be 1/16 of an inch thick and three to four inches long. At times, they may be seen looking like white threads in the dog's stool. These worms can suck blood from your dog at the rate of approximately a thimbleful per adult worm per week. Heavy infestations can, and frequently do, cause death to puppies. If you pull down the lower eyelid and examine the membrane within, a dog infected with Hookworm frequently has very pale membranes. His gums may also be much lighter in color than normal. This is due to the functional anemia caused by the worms sucking his blood. Hookworms also give off a toxin which may cause a puppy to appear to have fits. These are transitory and provided the condition (i.e., the Hookworm) is cleared up in time, no permanent damage will result. Because of the anemia caused by the worms, it is frequently desirable to add a little iron to the diet to counteract the deficiency. Hookworm, too, can be readily eliminated

Hookworms!

PURINA PET CARE CENTER

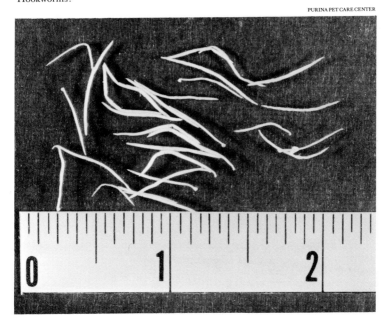

217

either by a worm capsule or with an injection given by your veterinarian.

Tapeworms

Tapeworms are long, flat worms composed of many segments, like links of flattened sausages. The rear segments carrying the eggs frequently drop off and are passed out with the bowel movement. They look like flattened brown or pink grains of rice in the hair around the anus or in the feces. It is a popular belief that Tapeworms cause an enormous increase in a dog's appetite, but actually, the reverse is true. The presence of Tapeworms depresses the appetite, frequently causing a run-down appearance and, at times, coughing. Because of the way they are passed, Tapeworms eggs are frequently not seen by the veterinarian when he examines the stool of the dog to determine the presence of parasites. So it is up to the dog owner to keep a sharp eye on his dog to detect the presence of these parasites as they are passed, at which time they are clearly visible.

Tapeworm!

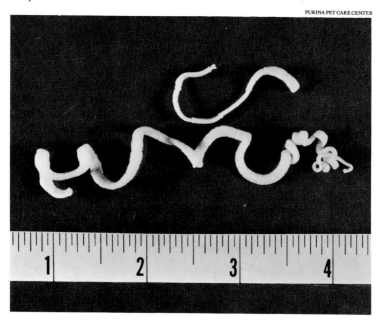

Tapeworms require an intermediate host which is in this case the flea. The flea larva feeds on the Tapeworm segments and then when the flea matures and becomes parasitic on the dog, the dog swallows the flea and the whole cycle begins again. The flea bite itself does not pass the eggs from flea to dog. The easiest and most practical way to prevent your dog from becoming infected with Tapeworms is to keep him free of fleas.

Medication is available. It is a little more difficult to treat than the other types of worms.

Fleas, Ticks and Lice

Not too long ago, it was believed that fleas, lice and ticks were unavoidable adjuncts to keeping a dog. Today we know better. There are many powders, sprays, dips, as well as medications which can be given internally, to eliminate these tormenting and frequently harmful pests. There is no excuse for keeping a parasite ridden dog. To eliminate these pests, we should know a little about them, how to recognize them, how they infect a dog, and their life cycle so that we can bring it to an end.

Ctenocephalides canis

CHET PLEGGE, D.V.M.

The flea!

Fleas

Fleas are probably the most frequently encountered external parasite. We have all heard the expression "As common as fleas on the belly of a hound dog." This need not and should not be true today. Fleas can really hurt a dog. They are the cause of Tapeworm.

Fleas are tiny black insects that infest the coat of your pet. Hidden by the hair they are frequently not discovered until they have proliferated. Then, when the hair is parted, they are seen scurrying for cover. Difficult to catch and hard-shelled, they can make tremendous leaps. An indication of their presence is sores on the belly, resembling mosquito bites on a human being. Flea droppings looking like black specks will be seen on the dog's skin.

Both male and female fleas infest dogs. The big ones are female; the small ones male. The female lays eggs which drop off on the ground or floor, in a rug, floor cracks, or upholstered furniture. When these eggs hatch, a worm emerges, spins a cocoon and pupates, to emerge as a flea which jumps on the first warm body that passes by. The warm body may even be a human. (While it may be a blow to human vanity, the flea really prefers the dog, and although dog fleas have been known to bite humans, they much prefer their canine hosts.)

Vacationers returning home with their pet to a closed-up house are often astonished to find it infested with fleas. As you can realize from this brief description of their life cycle, these are from the eggs laid before the dog left the house. They have hatched and are waiting for their "warm body."

It follows then, to deflea a dog properly and keep him free of the pests, it is not only necessary to destroy the fleas on the animal but also those in his surroundings. There are a number of commercial products on the market especially prepared for the elimination of fleas. For a heavy infestation, a bath, followed by a good flea dip, is recommended. Afterward, dust the dog thoroughly with a recommended flea powder and he will become a walking flea trap, poisoning any flea unfortunate enough to encounter him. Since fleas are great travelers, moving from one end of the dog to the other, for routine prevention measures it is merely necessary to spray one or two areas of the dog.

At the same time, use an insecticide to fumigate his surroundings — wherever he is accustomed to lie or sleep.

The latest and simplest method of flea control is by the use of a new pesticide with the trade name, Vapona. It can be purchased in resin strips about ten inches long which are hung close to the dog, either in the house or in the kennel. The resin is impregnated with an insecticide whose fumes kill any fleas that breathe its odor. The smell is completely unobjectionable to human noses. Vapona is also the active ingredient of the "90 Day" ™ dog collar which, when worn by the dog 24 hours a day, keeps him free of fleas for a period of three months. It also helps in the control of ticks.

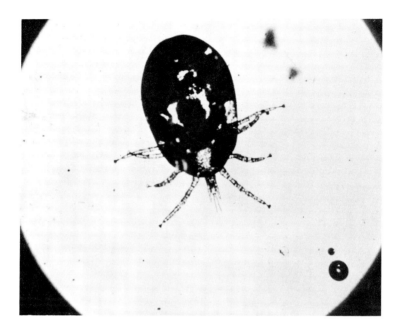

A photomicrograph of the common dog tick.

Ticks

At one time ticks were found primarily in southern areas. But in recent times, as world weather seems to have grown milder, they have moved northward. Today they are even a problem in Canada. The two most common types are the Brown Tick and the American Dog Tick. The American Dog Tick is primarily a parasite of the countryside, while the Brown Tick is found inside buildings. Only the female is parasitic. The male — an insignificant flat creature — is usually found under the engorged body of the female.

The female tick too, is an insignificant flat creature but only until she attaches herself to your pet, sinking her mouthparts into his skin. There she sucks blood until she swells up to the size of a small grape. This is when you'll spot her, frequently inside your dog's ears, or on his neck. On a long-haired dog ticks may be felt if not seen while you are petting or grooming it.

To remove a tick touch it with a cotton swab dipped in alcohol. Then use a tweezer to pull the parasite off. Be careful to take hold of it as close to the dog's body as possible so that it does not break when you pull it off. Don't be alarmed if you pull a tiny bit of the dog's skin off with it since this is better than leaving the mouthparts embedded in the dog. Dab the "wound" with peroxide. Destroy the tick; otherwise, it will recover and reinfect the dog.

If a female tick is not removed and destroyed, she will gorge herself on blood and then drop off the dog and crawl into a protected area where she will lay as many as 6000 eggs. Her life cycle completed, she dies. But the eggs, going through their cycle, will produce young which, like the flea, will climb up onto plants and wait for an animal host to come along.

The Brown Tick which seems to prefer—as we mentioned before—buildings, frequently infests houses and even apartments. Sometimes it is brought in on potted plants. Fortunately, they will not live on humans, preferring the dog as their host. However, once Brown Ticks have infested a house they are difficult to get rid of — the services of a professional exterminator may be necessary.

There are powders, sprays and dips available for treating ticks, and

A photomicrograph of a louse.

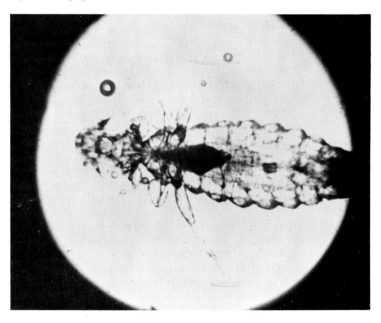

as we mentioned when discussing fleas, the Vapona treated collar helps. Ordinary flea products will not do. Any commercial product used should specify on the label that it eliminates ticks.

It is well to keep in mind that any insecticidal spray, for animals or plants, and not intended specially for pet care, should never be used on your dog. Such sprays contain products that are toxic to pets. Nor should a dog medication ever be used on a cat.

Lice

The louse lives its entire life on the dog — it does not, like the flea, go elsewhere to lay its eggs. These you will see on the dog — nits as they are called — fastened to the hairs; they resemble tiny silver globules. Infection is by direct contact. There are two types — sucking and biting. Some are red, some gray, some bluish. The sucking louse, like the tick, sucks blood. The biting louse feeds on skin scales and other matter. Lice are difficult to eliminate. Use a dip prescribed for them and then sprinkle the animal with an insecticide. Usually several dips at 10 to 12 day intervals are necessary. These nits are extremely resistant.

Skin Ailments

Slow, rhythmic scratching in one particular place (or places) indicates a skin infection or irritation. Examine the dog carefully, parting the coat with a comb, until you discover those spots where the skin is bare or inflamed. There are several brands of antiseptic powder which help to alleviate simple skin disorders. You may want to try one of these if the ailment is in its early stage; but as skin complaints spread rapidly, have a variety of causes, and are notoriously hard to cure, my recommendation is to seek professional advice and save yourself, not to mention the dog, a long and trying experience.

Ringworm

Ringworm is not a worm at all but a fungus which attacks dogs and cats as well as human beings. It can be passed back and forth from animals to man. Sores appear more often on the ears, face, neck, and tail than on other parts of the body. Since the hair is not shed, the infected areas may be overlooked for some time. As the infection spreads, the patches get larger and become incrusted.

Treatment: Cut away the hair from the lesions, remove the incrusted material with mineral oil and a cotton swab and apply a recommended ringworm cure. Sometimes tincture of iodine will bring it under control. Since Ringworm can be caught by humans, it is advisable to seek professional help and to wear gloves and be especially careful when treating the animal. Never let a child play with a dog suffering from Ringworm, or vice versa.

Eczema

This, a common skin ailment, is sometimes mistaken for Ringworm or mange. It seems to have a number of causative agents—allergy, fungi, fleas, and chiggers as well as faulty diet. It is characterized by intense itching, dandruff, loss of hair, sores and scabs. There are two types, moist and dry, with moist more often affecting the Shepherd. Treatment: Wash the affected parts with soap and water — a medicated soap like Dial is good, and apply a recommended lotion or ointment. Chronic cases should be turned over to the vet.

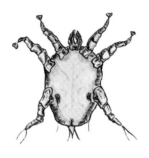

Otodectes cynotis

CHET PLEGGE, D.V.M.

The ear mite!

Mange

There are several types of mange. If you suspect one, have your vet take a scraping of the affected skin and examine it under a microscope. Only he can determine which type it is.

Ear Mange (Otodectic), sometimes called canker, is caused by rather large mites which infect the ear canal, causing painful irritation. The dog repeatedly shakes his head and scratches, crying and whining meanwhile. Soak a layer of cotton in mineral oil, wrap it around your index finger, and clean the ear with this gently.

There are many excellent cures for ear canker but scrupulous cleanliness helps most of all. The gray wax that accumulates in the ear canals will warn you of the mite's presence if the dog's misery and scratching at the base of the ear has not already pointed it out. Quite often a dog has been deemed " crabby" or shy when all that ailed him was ear mange.

Sarcoptic Mange Mite

Demodectic Mange Mite

CHET PLEGGE, D.V.M.

Sarcoptic and Demodectic Mange

This should be treated at once as secondary bacterial infections may occur. These are greatly to be dreaded as they may take three months or more to cure, and treatment involves using medicated baths and lotions. Red, angry patches with crusts on them are found on the inner sides of the flanks, belly and legs. In warm weather the skin exudes a stale, mouse like smell. The irritation is considerable, and as the infection is transmissible to human beings (Scabies), Sarcoptic mange must be placed under professional care at once.

Demodectic mange is not too common. It usually manifests itself on the face, head, or legs in bare patches with the affected skin dark in color and very thin and poor. It, too, is difficult to treat and may take several months to clear up. Bitches can pass this ailment on to their litters even though they appear healthy themselves. Professional treatment is required.

To avoid the possibility of "dog poisoners," teach your dog to refuse food offered by strangers.

XVII   First Aid

The dog owner should familiarize himself with this section ahead of time so that he will already know what to do in the event of an emergency. This is not to say that accidents happen frequently to dogs: they do not. The average city dog may go through life without ever having a call of an emergency nature.

First aid is front line treatment. It is intended to care for or relieve the pain or problem until professional help can be obtained. Accidents frequently occur at times or at places when a veterinarian is not available. So, in the unlikely event that something should happen, be prepared.

Restraint

A dog suffering from pain and bewildered because of the suddenness

226

of an accident may, on occasion, revert to a semi-wild state. This is particularly true if the dog does not know you, but it can happen with your own beloved pet. Approach the dog gently, speaking soothingly, watching his eyes and head for any sign of response. Should he snarl, bare his teeth or attempt to bite, it is best to improvise a muzzle. This can be a strip of cloth about two inches wide and approximately three feet long. In an emergency, a stocking or necktie will do. A loose loop is formed in the center, and tossed over his jaws, then drawn tight with the knot under his chin. The loose ends are drawn back around his head and knotted behind the ears. This will prevent him from biting. Now attempt to make him lie down by holding the nape of his neck and pulling his hind legs out from under him.

For large dogs it may be necessary to use a lasso. The noose is thrown over the dog's head, the loose end passed either between two boards and a fence, if outdoors; or through the crack between the door and door jam, if indoors. The dog is then drawn tight up against the stationary object while a muzzle is applied. If an assistant is available, two lassos can be used, with each person drawing one tight in opposite directions, thus immobilizing the dog. One lasso is tied to a solid object, and while the assistant controls the other one to restrain the dog, the muzzle can be applied.

The dog that continues to struggle, even after he has been muzzled, may be further restrained by tying his front legs and hind legs together. The object is to prevent him from doing damage to himself and to protect the person who is administering first aid. A small dog can frequently be restrained by tossing a blanket over him and gathering him up in that.

Broken Bones

This is probably the most common injury requiring emergency treatment. Broken bones are known as fractures and there are two types: simple fractures in which the bone is broken but the ends remain inside the skin of the body, and compound fractures, where the ends of the bones protrude through the skin. Of the two, the latter is far more serious but both types should be set by a skilled veterinarian as soon as possible.

It is frequently difficult to determine whether a dog's leg has been broken or merely injured, bruised, sprained or pulled. This is because when a dog feels pain in his leg he will limp regardless of how serious or trivial the cause. Feel the leg gently for suspicious bumps or dislocations. If in doubt, run your hand along the other leg at the same location to see whether the two feel the same. If there is any question in your mind, splint the leg until the services of a veterinarian can be obtained. He has X-ray equipment and will be in a better position to judge whether an actual break has occurred.

The simplest type of splint consists of two sticks (even broken tree branches will do in an emergency) which are laid on either side of the leg and then tied securely above and below the suspected break. This keeps the dog from moving or thrashing his leg about, causing the broken ends of bone to penetrate the skin and perhaps sever an important blood vessel. If medical supplies are at hand, it is best to wrap the leg in absorbent cotton before applying the splints. The splints can be held in place by putting additional layers of cotton about them and wrapping the entire leg carefully with a bandage. This makes a much more accurate splint and will hold the leg firmly in place until the bone can be set. Occasionally a dog's tail will be broken and the same procedure should be followed. It is not uncommon to see a dog with a kinked tail due to a break which was not set at the time of injury.

Sprains

Puppies are prone to sprains or strains — twisting a leg when playing, falling in a hole — all sorts of things. You may well hear a frightful scream, rush to see what is the matter, and have your puppy " tell you" he has hurt his leg and will never be able to walk again. Take him away from his companions at once. Keep him alone and quiet, and very often after a short period you will find him perfectly all right. However, if this does not happen, there are various liniments and remedies, nearly all of them to be found in the family medicine chest.

Bandaging your dog can present a problem because he may try to tear the bandage off. If he does, spread hot mustard over the outside; it should end any idea he may have of chewing it. However, there are dogs who like the taste of mustard; in their case I suggest bitter aloes.

If the dog seems to be in pain after a bandage has been applied, check that it is not on too tight; for although it may have been on right when applied, it is possible for an injured part to swell, causing the bandage to tighten and cut off blood circulation.

Bruises

A dog does not seem to suffer as easily from bruising as does a human being. The best advice is to give the dog rest and to keep the bruised area cool by the application of either ice packs or cold compresses. Unless a bone has been chipped, this treatment will usually suffice. If the swelling fails to subside in three or four days, best have it X-rayed.

Eye Accidents

It is all too easy for a dog to injure his eye. Puppy may scratch puppy; an adult dog in training or play can very easily run onto a spike or a sharp twig.

If your dog comes to with an eye closed and watering, examine it for a foreign body. This is usually easy to deal with. Hold the dog's head slightly to one side, and raise its lower eyelid a little; just enough to make a tiny cup. Into this pour lukewarm water or cold tea, and try to flush out the object. If this fails, take the dog to your veterinarian as quickly as you can before the foreign body does more injury.

A scratch on the eye is another matter; the best thing to use is an ophthalmic ointment containing an antibiotic (a prescription is required). Put it into the eye and take your dog to the veterinarian. If no ointment is at hand, wash the eye out with lukewarm water before rushing the dog to the vet.

Stings

A puppy chasing a lazy bee or even a wasp, which he will consider a grand thing to play with, may well end up with a nasty sting. Remember that a bee leaves its sting in the animal; a wasp does not. Stings on the muzzle, ear, tongue, eye and throat are quite common. Stings in the throat (when the insect is swallowed) are particularly dangerous because if the throat swells up it may cause suffocation. If your dog is stung and the spot starts to swell, try to find the sting and remove it with tweezers. Then apply cut onion, or a thick paste of bicarbonate of soda. If the sting is in the mouth, it is not necessary to make a paste, just rub the soda on. Watch your dog until you are quite certain that the swelling is not increasing. If it does, particularly if in the mouth or throat, take him to your veterinarian at once; an injection can be given that will relieve it. Sometimes an antihistamine pill will quickly reduce the swelling.

Snake Bites

Few areas of the world outside of the frigid zones are completely free of poisonous snakes. Australia has many species. The United States has rattlesnakes, copperheads, cottonmouth moccasins and in the deep South, coral snakes.

If the poisonous venom is introduced directly into an artery by a snake's bite, the dog usually dies. But if the bite is in the muscle or the feet, there is usually time to get your dog to the nearest veterinarian who will inject him with anti-venom and the chances are good for recovery. If possible pack the area with ice.

A quickly improvised tourniquet placed about the leg above the bite will help. It will cause so much discomfort that the dog will try to tear it off, so he should be muzzled.

The X cuts over the punctures to induce bleeding are no longer used. Instead it is best to cut a small area over and around the puncture and apply suction.

Wounds

Dogs are easily wounded—minor cuts, scratches, or bites from another dog—but these rarely require treatment because the dog's tongue will usually do all that is necessary to keep such wounds clean until they heal. A wound that bleeds freely is generally safe because it will rid itself of poisons. The kind of wound which can be dangerous is a deep puncture wound which bleeds little or not at all, and tends to heal from the surface inwards, trapping bacteria and becoming septic at a later stage. This type of wound should be kept open until it appears absolutely clean and healthy.

Before bandaging any wound, make sure there is no foreign body in it. If there is, do your very best to extract it. If you cannot do so, get professional help. Wounds should be bathed with a mild antiseptic solution after the hair has been cut away from the area. Antibiotic ointments, although obtainable only on prescription, are excellent for all wounds so it is wise to get some from your vet to keep in your medicine chest. A large cut may need suturing, and for this, of course, you will have to see your vet. If a wound is bleeding excessively, it may be necessary to apply a tourniquet, or to stop the bleeding with a pressure bandage.

Tourniquet

Cuts in the legs frequently bleed far out of proportion to the actual injury. However, any extensive loss of blood is, of course, dangerous and a tourniquet should be applied. Any piece of strong cloth or cord can be used to make a tourniquet — even a handkerchief or a necktie. Before applying a tourniquet, decide whether the blood is coming from a vein or an artery. Arterial blood will be bright red and come out in a pulsing beat; venous blood is dark and flows more steadily. It is important to determine which type of blood vessel has been cut, because to stop arterial bleeding you must apply the tourniquet between the cut and the heart; whereas to stop the flow of blood from the vein, the tourniquet should be applied on the far side of the cut from the heart.Take your piece of cord or cloth and tie it around the limb loosely, tying a knot. A small piece of stick is then inserted through the loop and twisted to tighten the cord until the flow of blood stops. The tourniquet should be loosened every five to ten minutes; otherwise loss of circulation will damage the leg.

Pressure Bandage

A pressure bandage is a bandage applied over the injury firmly enough to stop the flow of blood. Apply a pad of absorbent cotton to the affected area. Wrap this tightly with regular gauze bandage and then cover the area with adhesive tape to keep the dog from chewing it off. If it is applied tightly enough, it will stop the bleeding. Inexperienced people frequently apply pressure bandages without tightening them enough to do the job for which they are intended. Because of this necessary tightness, such bandages should not be left on for more than 15 to 20 minutes. But if applied to the foot a pressure bandage can be left in place for as long as thirty minutes without harm.

Shock

A dog in any accident, especially one that involves a blow to the head, or one in which some vital organ is damaged or ribs broken, will generally, mercifully, go into shock. He is less conscious of pain, but his condition is often frightening, his pulse and respiration slow and often shallow. He may feel cold to the touch, pant, have a rapid pulse and exhibit extreme thirst.

Don't try to apply heat. The best treatment is to cover the dog with blankets and let his own body heat build up. Don't try to move him, unless the weather is extremely cold, or unless he is in direct sun which is too hot. In that case, place an open blanket on the ground alongside him and try to roll or slide him onto it; then using the blanket as a stretcher, carry him to a more suitable location, or to where he can obtain professional help. Should he seem conscious and desirous of drinking, you may spoon feed him, but very slowly to allow him to swallow naturally. Make some instant coffee — such as you would drink yourself — Karo or honey — 75 % coffee to 25 % syrup — and a pinch of salt. Try to hold his head up so that he can swallow naturally, but if he struggles or resists swallowing, discontinue feeding. The caffeine in coffee is a natural stimulant but a mild one, and the syrup contains glucose to provide extra energy.

While he is in shock you may be able to get him to a veterinarian who will be able to sedate him; as the state of shock disappears, the dog becomes more conscious of pain.

If a puppy is in shock, pick him up by holding one hand under his front, and the other under his hindquarters. This will help to keep him stretched out.

Artificial Respiration

After an accident, a dog is sometimes unable to breathe. Should yours be in this condition, first pull his tongue out, and, if he is unconscious, wipe out his throat using cotton or a handkerchief. Feel for a heartbeat and if you can detect it, try gently pressing on the rib cage and quickly releasing the pressure. Repeat many times, rhythmically, about twenty times to the minute. Stop as soon as you see or feel him breathing normally. This procedure has saved many a dog.

Collapse

Collapse usually occurs in an old dog. It may happen on a very hot day; if it does, move him to the coolest place you can find, making sure he is in a current of fresh air. Check that his tongue is clear of his windpipe; pull it out of his mouth, and let it hang so that there is no chance of his swallowing it. Raise him and keep his head a little lower than his body, and send for your veterinarian.

Should the collapse occur in cold weather, keep the dog as warm as possible while awaiting the arrival of your vet; take the same precautions with his tongue.

Electric Shock

The wire on the floor offers temptation to any dog and especially to puppies. If your puppy persists in going behind the furniture or remaining quietly out of sight, check and make sure that he is not lying there gnawing on a live wire. If he chews through the insulation, his mouth will be badly burned, sometimes severely. He may urinate, and if he is standing close to a metal conductor which the urine touches he may well be electrocuted.

If this happens, keep away from the urine and shut off the switch which feeds the wire. If you rush to his aid without taking this precaution you, too, may be electrocuted. If you cannot for some reason shut off the current, use a dry wooden object to remove the wire from the dog's mouth, or to push the dog away from the live wire. If he has stopped breathing, try giving artificial respiration, as explained above. He will probably be in shock. Treat him accordingly. If his tongue or lips are burned, take him to the doctor. Remember, puppies and exposed wires do not go well together, so try always to keep them apart.

Drowning

This is rare. German Shepherds swim naturally and have no problem in the water. However, they sometimes fall or are pushed off a height and the impact either with the water or an object in the water can render them unconscious, and they drown. Another cause of accidental drowning is when children play with big dogs and try to ride them or climb on their backs in the water.

The first thing to do is to pull out the dog's tongue and shake his head in a lowered position to drain out as much excess water as possible. As soon as possible, apply artificial respiration; this will frequently save a life. The important thing is to sense the urgency. Deliberate speed may very well determine whether your dog lives or dies.

Heat Stroke

The only appreciable way a dog has of reducing his temperature is by evaporating water from his throat, tongue, and footpads. He has few sweat glands. That is why a dog pants, and when extremely hot, salivates as well. As the water evaporates, he becomes cool at the point of evaporation. To reduce a dog's temperature to normal, we must put this principle to work.

Suppose you find your dog panting and slobbering in a state of collapse? How do you give first aid? The quickest way is to put him in the bathtub and run cold water over him. Should there be no bathtub available, you may use a hose, and, lacking even that, dashing a bucket of cold water over him will help. With the dog thoroughly soaked, try to provide circulation of air around him. An electric fan is probably the best, but again, if this is not available, a cardboard or flapping towel, or even a newspaper used as a fan will keep the air moving and help reduce his body temperature. The important thing is not to slacken in your efforts until the dog shows definite signs of recovery.

Should you be driving at the time heat prostration strikes—a frequent occurrence—lay the dog on the floor of the front seat, wet him down and keep the hood ventilator open to let the air flow over him while you drive. Continue to pour enough water over his body to keep him damp on the way to help. If you are driving across a hot desert area and your dog can't stand heat, be sure to prepare yourself in advance with containers of water.

The important thing to remember is to get the dog out of the heated area as soon as possible into a shaded place and to circulate air around him while wetting him down.

Fish Hooks

It is not unusual for a dog to be hooked, particularly when a lure is snapped back preparatory to casting. Do not try to pull the hook back out of the skin the way it entered, as the barb will tear the flesh. Fortunately, most fishing boxes contain hook-cutting pliers. Should none be available at the moment, cut the line fastened to the hook, and try to keep the dog from struggling until pliers can be obtained. Cut the shank of the hook as close to the skin as possible, and pull each half out. The wound can be treated as indicated under *Wounds*.

Splinters

When you see your dog limping, examine the pads, particularly the spaces between, for splinters or thorns which may have become embedded. If the end is visible, tie the dog's mouth so that he cannot snap from pain, and pull the object out with a strong pair of tweezers by taking a firm grip on the splinter as close to the flesh as you can. If it does not come right out, removing it is a job for the veterinarian. Splinters left in the flesh too long can cause Tetanus (Lockjaw), especially if pus develops. Your dog's doctor will decide whether to give an antitoxin.

Not all splinters enter the feet. The dog will point out the offender when he tries to pull it out.

Skunk Spray

Dogs allowed to wander freely, even in the suburbs, frequently meet a skunk, with the inevitable result. While it is true that time and weather will take care of the odor, the dog, who will be a bit upset and come galloping home, cannot be allowed to remain in his odorous state about the house. Frequently, the eyes are irritated by the spray. Fortunately, skunk spray causes only local irritation — never blindness.

To remove the odor, wash your dog with a detergent, rinse him well and then rub canned tomato or orange juice into the coat. Allow it to soak in for at least ten minutes, then rebathe him with a strong detergent, and rinse. You may have to repeat this procedure several times because, no doubt about it, skunk odor lingers!

Porcupine Quills

Dogs sometimes encounter porcupines and end up stuck with quills. It usually happens in a place far from veterinary help. So if you are going into woods known to be porcupine country better take along a pair of electricians pliers. First chain the dog and hold him standing while you pull the quills from one side — pull! no matter how painful. He can then be laid on that side. Work on his mouth next, and his tongue. Then around his eyes. Next behind the shoulders and the belly to prevent quills from working into vital organs. Consider this merely first aid. Get the dog to the vet, as fast as possible. Quills that work themselves in will have to be removed under anesthetic.

Poisoning

When poisoning is suspect, the first thing to do is to determine the kind of poison involved. For instance, if you see your pet dig up mole bait, quickly locate the container and read the formula. Only when you know your poison can you supply the proper antidote. The wrong antidote can even intensify the poison's effect. But in almost all cases, the first thing to do is to empty the dog's stomach while someone else phones the vet for advice. (Many of the larger cities have Poison Control Centers. They are listed in the phone book — if not call your Department of Health — and in an emergency they will give you advice over the phone.)

Hydrogen peroxide is an excellent — and usually handy — emetic. Use a 3% solution (this is the common household strength) mixed half and half with water. A German Shepherd will need about half a glassful to produce results. Make a lip pocket and hold his head upward. Pour the solution in and rub his throat so he swallows. Try to get him to swallow the entire amount. Vomiting occurs in about two minutes.

Some poisons are corrosive. They burn what they touch: mouth, throat, gullet, stomach. In these cases, unless antidotes are given almost immediately, it is too late. Because the stomach contains fluid, the damage by some acids and alkalis is not quite so immediate. The way to counteract their action is to try to keep the poisons from corroding deeper into tissue and to neutralize them.

Once an area has been damaged, it requires a long time to heal. The dog may be unable to eat for weeks, yet continue to live. Any treatment given while the dog is recuperating must take this into consideration. Here are some of the more common poisons:

> **Alkalis:** *The most frequent one is drain cleaner. When cleaning drains some of the left-over caustic is frequently thrown into the garbage. It takes only a few crystals to cause damage.* **Symptoms:** *Intense salivation, often followed by nausea and vomiting, and expression of pain.* **Treatment:** *Neutralize the caustic by giving vinegar or lemon juice.*
>
> **Garbage Poisoning:** *Partially decomposed food in which food poisoning organisms have developed can be deadly, but there is often time to save the dog.* **Symptoms:** *Usually trembling is the first sign, followed by prostration. When botulin poisoning is the*

cause, the dog becomes slack all over as if he lacked strength in his muscles, especially the neck. Frequently he is unable to vomit voluntarily. **Treatment:** Empty the stomach with peroxide diluted 50-50 with water, and when the nausea has ended, give Epsom salts or another quick acting laxative.

Cyanide: Many cyanide poisonings are deliberate, but not always. Because so many suburbanites are troubled by ground moles, thousands of packages of mole poisons are sold annually. The property owner buries them in burrows to kill the moles. But, unfortunately, curious dogs see or smell the place where the ground has been freshly dug, scratch up the mole poison and eat it. Many mole poisons contain cyanide, but not enough of it to be immediately fatal. **Symptoms:** If you think your dog has swallowed cyanide, take a sniff of his breath — the odor of almonds may be smelled. Look to see if his gums and tongue are blue. He will show pain, and have trouble breathing. **Treatment:** Give peroxide (50-50) with water; you may save him. But let your veterinarian carry on from there.

Warfarin: This most common of all rat poisons, fortunately for dog owners, must be eaten three or four times to cause death. Death is caused by internal bleeding. Even two times will cause some ill effects. **Symptoms:** Paleness of the gums, lips and tongue. General overall weakness. **Treatment:** In the early stages, simply keeping the dog away from warfarin will help him to recover. In the last stages, no treatment is known. Transfusions have been given but they produce only temporary improvement. Consult your veterinarian. In time, an antidote or more effective treatment may be discovered.

Phosphorus: Another common rodent poison. Its effects on dogs are cruel. **Symptoms:** Often causes writhing pain. The breath has a garlic odor; diarrhea begins rapidly; the dog first becomes prostrated, goes into a coma and dies. **Treatment:** Phosphorus circulating in the bloodstream damages internal organs. The quickest possible treatment is essential. Peroxide, mixed with water (50-50) is the antidote; as we saw, it also causes vomiting. Even though you save your dog's life, it may be a long time before he will act like his old self.

Thallium: One of the common insect and rodent poisons. It is a slow poison with symptoms sometimes developing days after ingestion, at which time only supportive veterinary treatment is *effective.* **Symptoms:** *when large amounts have been ingested, salivation and drooling, nausea and vomiting, diarrhea expressions of pain.* **Treatment:** *a solution of table salt given as quickly as possible.*

Paint: *This is a broad term. The active poisons are the pigments used in paint formulas and the lead in the white lead which gives paint substance and adhesive properties. Paris green is sometimes used as a pigment. This is an arsenical. Any dog that licks fresh green paint should be considered a possible poison victim and be properly treated. The lead in the paint (if it is a lead-base paint) will complicate the problem.* **Symptoms:** *telltale paint around the dog's muzzle and lips, or even on the body, should make one suspicious He will exhibit pain in the abdomen, perhaps tremble, breathe rapidly, and constantly move about until he becomes prostrate.*

Treatment: *Empty the stomach, and when the nausea has subsided give a teaspoonful of Epsom salts in water. The lead is less dangerous, but the arsenic in the paris green may, if much has been absorbed, lengthen the convalescence period.*

Strychnine: *Those who use strychnine to poison foxes or other varmints not infrequently accidentally poison dogs. But, like cyanide, strychnine poisoning is sometimes done maliciously.*

Symptoms: *The typical violent twitching and trembling, with short periods of quiet, can never be forgotten by anyone who has seen a dog with strychnine poisoning. These tremblings usually end in death, depending on the quantity of poison consumed.*

Treatment: *If you can get your dog to the veterinarian alive, chances are that he can save him. He will inject a drug that will counteract the trembling and empty the stomach.*

If you happen to have some sleeping capsules—one of the barbiturates (1 1/2 gr.) such as phenobarbital, Nembutal or Seconal, dissolve the contents of five or six (if the dog is an adult German Shepherd) in a little water, and administer it by the lip-pocket method. Then hurry to the veterinarian.

Copper: *Copper is occasionally eaten in the form of copper sulphate. Dogs chew corroded areas on copper pipes and become sick. Ingredients in some spray materials are also copper sulphate.* **Symptoms:** *Expressions of pain, sometimes convulsions, twitching; and after a lapse of time the dog may void blue-colored stools.* **Treatment:** *Use diluted peroxide to* induce vomiting if you can treat the pet immediately, and then get him to the vet's — fast.

Plant Sprays: Today these consist of a wide variety of chemicals, and new ones are coming on the market every year. For some there are no antidotes. The old sprays were mostly arsenicals or copper sulphate, discussed above.

Insect Sprays: For DDT there is no published antidote.

Chlordane: Sprinkled on lawns or gardens to kill grubs, or spread around the foundations of homes to eradicate termites, chlordane is an ever present danger. It is a slower poison than some. If you can't get to a veterinarian at once, induce vomiting with diluted peroxide.

Sodium Fluoride: This is sprinkled on floors and shelves of closets to destroy roaches and ants. Dogs often drop bones or meat on it, then eat the meat and are poisoned. Induce vomiting with peroxide in water, and get your dog to the vet.

Ant Cups or Buttons: These are used to rid premises of annoying pests. Ant cups are metal bottle caps filled with a sweetened, poisoned material. Dogs often chew them, sometimes swallowing the caps along with the poison. They are usually made with thallium or arsenic so read the contents on the package label and give the proper antidote. Fortunately, both of these poisons are now being replaced with safer ones.

Radiator Antifreeze: It is often ethylene glycol. It may drip from a leak, and since it tastes sweet, dogs are tempted to lap it up. It changes to oxalic acid which does the real poisoning. **Symptoms:** Chiefly pain and nausea. **Treatment:** If you are sure the dog has lapped antifreeze, empty his stomach with diluted peroxide, and give a teaspoonful of bicarbonate of soda dissolved in water; then consult your veterinarian.

Chocolate: The theobromine in black cooking chocolate, similar to caffeine in coffee, is highly concentrated. Many dogs have stolen and eaten bars of this chocolate which, while it may not have proved fatal, produced violent shaking. **Treatment:** Empty the stomach with diluted peroxide and if you have any barbiturate sleeping pills dissolve the contents of several in an ounce of water. Don't exceed a 1 1/2 grain capsule for each ten pounds of the dog's weight. Administer by the lip-pocket method. Then let your veterinarian carry on. He may inject a sedative intravenously and quickly counteract the nervous symptoms. Be sure to tell him what medication you have already given.

Laurel and Rhododendron Leaves: *It is surprising how often dogs have been poisoned by these plants. No one has been able to discover the attraction.* **Symptoms:** *Nausea soon develops. There is profuse salivation and a general weakness.* **Treatment:** *Even if you know the dog has vomited, induce more vomiting with a peroxide mixture. Follow with Epsom salts for a laxative.*

Sleeping Pills: *It may surprise you to learn that many dogs somehow manage to find and eat sleeping pills. They must swallow them whole or the bitterness would cause the drug to be rejected.* **Symptoms:** *Should your dog for no apparent reason go into a deep sleep, suspect barbiturate poisoning.* **Treatment:** *Before he is too deeply unconscious to swallow, empty his stomach with diluted peroxide and give him half a cup of strong black coffee. Then take him to the veterinarian.*

Choking

A dog may choke from an obstruction in his throat. If it is high up in the throat, suffocation may follow very quickly, so action is essential. Open the dog's mouth and try to pull out whatever has become lodged. If you fail, try very gently to push the object further down. If it goes into the lower part of the throat, the risk of imminent death is over. It may mean that the object will have to be surgically removed later but at least you have a live dog from which to remove it. Other than this there is not much you can do in the case of the dog's choking. Take instant, speedy action.

Burns and Scalds

Unless the damaged area is slight, never attempt to treat a burn yourself. Cover the area with a loose bandage. Treat the dog for shock and take him at once to your vet. Your main object should be to exclude all air from the burnt area.

With German Shepherds, scalds are more difficult to treat than burns, because the dog's thick coat holds in the heat from the boiling liquid. The best thing is to slosh a pot of lukewarm water over the affected area. Never use cold water. This will only increase the after effects. Treat for shock and call in your veterinarian.

A 14 year old friend, still in excellent coat and health.

XVIII   Care of the Aged Dog

While ours is not considered a particularly long-lived breed there are many notable exceptions. Our longest-lived German Shepherd was a bitch who lived to 15 years and 9 months and retained her gorgeous shining coat until the end. We know many Shepherd dogs who are active and healthy twelve-year-olds and one "young" lady of 14 who has just returned bright eyed and bushy tailed from a rabbit hunt.

The secret of comfortable old age lies in diet control and daily exercise — although this should be less strenuous as the years advance — and particular care that the ageing dog sleeps and rests away from any drafts which could cause stiff muscles and painful rheumatism. A few extra sanitary measures are needed too, to keep a house dog pleasant to have around.

Reduce all starchy food to a minimum. One handful of wholewheat kibble as dry as possible, mixed with raw meat cut up smaller now, so that ageing teeth and tender gums can handle it comfortably. Two smaller meals may be easier on the digestion. Try giving the kibble with an egg yolk and a little warm milk and honey or Karo for breakfast, then feed a pound of raw meat in the evening, but nothing else. We find yogurt beneficial; since most dogs like cheese it is accepted eagerly. Beat natural, unsweetened yogurt with the same quantity of fresh milk and a teaspoonful of honey, and feed it for breakfast two or three times weekly instead of kibble and milk.

Give fresh vegetable juices only, or liquify carrots, parsley and watercress in an electric blender for easy assimilation. Vegetable bulk causes gas in weakened digestive systems. A supply of juice can be prepared twice a week and kept under refrigeration.

Feed only a little more than half the quantities suggested for an adult dog in his prime. Old dogs are sometimes very greedy and will start, after a lifetime of exemplary behavior, to beg (even steal) food. This "hunger" is caused by stomach irritation and acidity. Small and regular doses of milk of magnesia should be the rule from now on.

Check the teeth carefully and frequently for decay and for loose ones which the vet should remove. If the dog lives in the house, a couple of chlorophyll tablets will keep his breath pleasant. The very old dog's eliminations (particularly urine) are not always under control so it may be necessary to spread newspapers down at night as in puppyhood.

Deafness affects many dogs after about ten years, but if they live in familiar surroundings they are not unhappy. Even failing sight does not distress them if they are kept where they know their way around. Make sure that the ears are free of hard wax or any discharge.

Groom only with a medium soft brush, and use one of the many commercial dry shampoos. Bathing is dangerous to old dogs. Of course, advancing years tend to make a dog "crabby" when he is teased or pushed around by puppies or youngsters. So make sure he has a quiet place to rest that is not shut away and lonely, or he will pine away in his inactivity. Keep him near and dear as he deserves.

Euthanasia

If your old friend becomes very feeble or paralyzed in his

LOUISE VAN DER MEID

An older Shepherd likes to be with his master. Vicki feels particularly useful when carrying the groceries home.

The only true love that money can buy!

hindquarters, or if his natural functions get out of control and cause him distress after a lifetime of continence, *don't* keep him lingering until he dies of old age and in pain. This is sheer self-indulgence really, because none of us likes to face up to this terrible decision, but it must be made. Call your trusted vet and let him help your old friend to a peaceful and painless passing while your are feeding him some favorite morsel of food.

It is a thousand times better for the dog to go before real suffering begins, and only a selfish owner would think otherwise. When the dog is at rest, take a short trip or visit sympathetic friends. Then, if he was a " one and only," go off and buy another puppy as the finest tribute you can pay to your departed companion for his devotion and love for German Shepherds which he left in your heart.

APPENDIX

German Degrees: Their Meaning and How They are Earned

Germany has a great many degrees, which cover all the aspects of German Shepherd showing and competition. A knowledge of them is important for a full understanding of the background and organization on which the development of the German Shepherd was based. We would like to describe some of the ways degrees can be earned, since they are different from the American and English ones.

In Germany, a dog cannot be entered in the Adult classes (2 years and over) without working qualification. This means that the best bred dog is the one with the greatest number of working qualifications on his pedigree, since all his ancestors necessarily had to be qualified so that they could be put on exhibition. In this way it is clearly seen that intelligence and beauty march hand in hand with German stock, as it is impossible to make up a top winner in beauty without working qualifications and therefore strong character, as we will explain. A few breeders in outlying districts may not enter their stock at shows, which accounts for some otherwise excellent animals which do not have degrees after their names. In Germany, however, these are somewhat of an exception as interest is keen.

Since we are breeding Shepherd dogs, we will start the list with HGH. This degree can be won only by actual sheepherding dogs, for whom trials are held separately. These trials attract large numbers of spectators. The full title is *Herdengebrauchshund.*

The degree most commonly seen is the *Schützhund* (guard or defense dog) with the ratings I, II and III. The training and standard of work required to earn these degrees is extremely high; no dog who is gunshy *(Schusscheu)* has any time wasted on him. These are eliminated by testing at the start of the heel free exercise. Each grading has three separate divisions of nose work, obedience and man work. SchH I is for dogs from 14 months, while SchH II is for dogs from 16 months. The two tests are similar, with 100 being the maximum rating in each. SchH III is for dogs above the age of 20 months and is a very severe test. There is a compulsory wait of six weeks between competing for each grade. A dog failing to obtain a mark of 80 % in the manwork division must take the test again in order to qualify " good".

The heel work in the SchH III test is done off lead and also without commands from the judge or steward; the handler puts up a real show with his dog working heel free. This can often be seen in the Open class of the great Sieger Show, where one requirement is a demonstration of heel free handling which is always a delight to watch. In any case, you can be sure that any dog which has the above mentioned letters after his name is a thoroughly trained animal with a fearless character.

Another qualification which is frequently not understood is the word *"angekoert."* This rating is given to an animal at the *Koerung* (or Breed Survey). Here the dogs are submitted to a close and thorough examination, being weighed and measured, and with every small detail being noticed before being passed — or rejected — for breeding. This qualification also carries indications as to which blood lines blend suitably with the particular dog and which should be avoided, in order to prevent the perpetuation of faults on either side and hopefully to intensify the virtues. If this raises any question in your mind as to whether anyone troubles himself with what is written and recommended on a dog's report at the *Koerung*, we must assure you that no breeder would get very far if he ignored this vital guidance. In Germany, when a dog is judged, the handler must also present the dog's pedigree and all data for scrutiny, so that if he is not bred correctly he can never reach the top although he may be otherwise worthy of the honor.

Registration and Pedigree

A German Shepherd born in his own country is issued a really comprehensive document, on which there is detailed information of a kind unknown on the U.S. and British pedigrees; all the facts are checked with the S.V. headquarters so that there is no possible chance of a false pedigree being issued.

Since 1957, the registration certificate and pedigree *(Ahnentafel)* have been issued on pale green paper which is folded like a booklet into four pages. The first three contain all details about the dog which is registered thereon, while on the fourth page we find space for transfers of ownership *(Eigentumwechsel)*. The remainder is taken up with the rules and regulations of the S.V. Reading from the top of Page 1, you find the dog's name; sex *(Geschlecht);* color and distinguishing markings *(Farbe und Abzeichen)* with any particular characteristics *(Besondere Kennzeichen);* the date and month of birth *(Wurftag)* and year of birth, or more correctly of whelping *(Wurfjahr)*. The name of the breeder *(Züchter)* is also there. Under *Inzucht,* we find the line-breeding listed. There is also complete information about the other puppies in the litter *(Geschwister)* with their names and colors and other notes on the size of litter *(Wufrstärke)*, stating whether more than the six puppies permitted by the S.V. rules were raised and, if so, how many by the natural mother and how many by the foster mother.

Reading lower down on Page 1, there is a narrow rectangle in which are given the dog's registration number *(Nr)* and the volume *(Bd)* of the Stud Book *(Zuchtbuch)* in which he has been entered. There is a stern reminder that the pedigree is a legal document and that anyone who falsifies such a certificate can be prosecuted; and we are told, furthermore, that the pedigree belongs only to the dog himself and *must* be given to the new owner when the dog is sold.

This brings up an interesting point: In many countries the registering body for dogs is an agency of the government, and any falsification of pedigree is a crime punishable by the government. In the United States the registering body (American Kennel Club) is a private agency with no governmental police powers itself. They do excellent work in overseeing registration of dogs, and can refuse to register a dog, can revoke a registration, and can even refuse to register dogs of certain breedings or not to accept registrations from certain people. However, they cannot prosecute, except civilly. In the event of a fraud, evidence must be turned over to the authorities for appropriate action.

To return to the German pedigree: After this there is a space for notes or remarks *(Bemerkungen);* the date of issue *(Ausgefertigt);* and the signature *(Unterschrift)* of the breeder, to certify the authenticity of the foregoing information. Then, in another rectangle on the right of the bottom of this page, the S.V. state that they have examined the pedigree and certify it as correct, and give the date and serial number of the registration. To the left of this rectangle is a similar one, stating that the certificate must be validated by the S.V. for the life of the dog after he is 18 months old. You will see this validation in the form of a rubber stamp in red placed diagonally across this space of the words *Auf Lebenszeit verlängert,* meaning that it has been extended for life Before this extension can be obtained, the dog's owner must obtain a satisfactory report from a "young dog examiner" on the list of the S.V. or from a show where the dog has gained a rating of good *Gut* or higher for conformation. In the top right-hand corner of this page there is a space in which is entered the breed survey rating *(Koervermerke).* This could read, as an example, "*Angekoert* 1967-68 I," which tells us that the dog has been examined at the survey and passed for Class I, and is approved for breeding for those years. In the autumn of 1968 he would have to be presented again to the *Koermeister,* who may give an extension of the approval for a period of up to four years, which would bring the dog up to his eighth year. Should the dog be in good form at this age, he may be given a one year extension which is renewable for one year periods, year to year, but only after examination.

The difference between *Koerklasse* I and II is that the former denotes that the dog has a "special recommendation for breeding" whereas the latter classifies him as "suitable for breeding," indicating that he has one or two minor structural faults (or a missing premolar) but is otherwise approved for use by reason of good bloodlines or working performance. It happens sometimes that a dog improves sufficiently between examinations to be passed as Class I at a subsequent survey.

Unfolding the pedigree, on the inside pages 2 and 3 you will see a four generation pedigree of the dog, his parents *(Eltern)* and their parents back to the great, great grandparents *(Ur-Ur-Grosseltern)*. There is a wealth of useful information about all the dog's ancestors, including color and markings *(Farbe und Abzeichen)* and the survey reports *(Koerberichte)* of the two final generations together with a description of all the litter-mates of these six dogs with their names and training degrees, whether they have been surveyed, and their highest show rating if they have been shown. These pedigrees are literally a breeder's guide; and as all the information has been checked at the S.V. headquarters it is completely reliable and forms the basis of much useful knowledge in planning a litter or founding a kennel.

In the space of the right of page 3 there are full explanations of abbreviations and codes as follows: Z.B., standing for *Zucht-bewertung.* This is the rating received at a conformation show. Now we read about 20 abbreviations concerning color and markings, of which we give here the principal ones:

A	*Abzeichen*	*markings*
F	*Fang*	*muzzle or foreface*
L	*Laüfe*	*legs*
M	*Maske*	*mask*
PF	*Pfoten*	*feet or paws*
S	*Sattel*	*saddle*
b	*Braun*	*brown*
g	*Gelb*	*tan*
gr	*Grau*	*grey*
s	*Schwarz*	*black*

If the color-note reads sg, this means *schwarz und gelb,* i.e., black and tan; sgA means *schwarz mit gelben Abzeichen,* i.e., black with tan markings; sgrg is *schwarz-grau mit gelb,* i.e., black and grey with tan; while sggr stands for *schwarz-gelb mit grau,* which is black and tan with grey; sgrL means *schwarz mit grauen Laüfen* — black with grey legs; and sbAM stands for *schwarz mit braunen Abzeichen und Maske,* i.e., black with brown markings and muzzle. The predominant color is listed first, thus grg means grey with tan, and ggr means tan with grey. The whole range of colors is very thoroughly described; and one of the reasons for not stamping the dog's pedigree for life until he is 18 months old is that he may change color, which is frequently the case. We have seen sables turn black and tan and black dogs turn light golden sable — even a color blue, like a blue fox, may turn normal black and tan. Certainly the long and exact code of coloring is necessary and very well thought out.

Afterwards you have the long and complicated explanations of the various training qualifications, some of which are noted and described at the beginning of this chapter. The last part of this right-hand side of page 3 contains the grading or rating titles, which are as follows:

V-A	*Vorzüglich-Auslese*	*Excellent Select*
V	*Vorzüglich*	*Excellent*
S.G.	*Sehr Gut*	*Very Good*
G.	*Gut*	*Good*
AUSR.	*Ausreichend*	*Satisfactory*
M	*Mangelhaft*	*Faulty*
U	*Ungenügend*	*Unsatisfactory*
	("Null" is sometimes	
	noted instead of U)	

The top grading of V-A is only awarded to a small group of animals, perhaps six or eight of each sex, at the annual Sieger Show, the great National Specialty Show, where there may be up to 140 dogs in the Open class. It is therefore the crown of the breed, and only a practically faultless animal, with the best and most suited bloodlines behind it, and with 100 % Shepherd character can ever gain this highly coveted honor.

If the pedigree is written on pink colored paper, it signifies that both the dog's parents have been surveyed and passed fit for breeding, i.e., *Angekört*: and this pink document is known as a *Körzucht Ahnentafel.* Similarly, if both parents and all four grandparents of the dog have won training degrees, the pedigree is stamped *"Leistungszucht,"* which means breeding from dogs with training accomplishments.

GLOSSARY

An understanding of German descriptive terms is useful when reading show reports in the *S.V. Zeitung*, stud books or the pedigrees of imported stock.

Abzeichen (A)	Markings
Ahnen	Ancestors
Ahnentafel	Pedigree
Allgemeine Erscheinung	General Appearance
Alter	Age
Altersklasse (AK)	Adult Class
Angekört	Certified suitable for breeding
Augen	Eyes
Ausdruck	Expression
Bauch	Belly
Befriedigend (B)	Fair
Behaarung	Coat
Belegt	Bred
Besitzer	Owner
Bewertung	Qualification
Blau	Blue-grey
Braun (br)	Brown
Breit	Broad
Brust (Br)	Breast, Chest
Deckfarbe	Predominant Color
Drahthaarig	Wire coated
Dunkel (d)	Dark
Ehrenpreis	Prize of Honor
Eltern	Parents
Eng	Narrow
Enkel, Enkelin	Grandson, Granddaughter
Erziehung	Upbringing, Training
Farbe	Color
Fassbeine	Bowlegged
Fassrippe	Barrel-ribbed
Flanke	Loin
Flüchtig	Fleet
Futterzustand	Fine Condition
Gang	Gait
Gelb (g)	Gold, Tan
Gelbgrau (ggr)	Tan/grey sable
Geschlechtsgepräge	Sex-quality
Gesundheit	Sound health
Gewölkt	Dingy, mixed colors
Gewinkelt	Angulated
Geworfen	Whelped
Glatthaarig	Smooth coated
Graugelb (grg)	Greyish tan (sable)
Gross	Large
Grosseltern	Grandparents
Gut (G)	Good
Hals	Throat, Neck
Harmonisch	Co-ordinated
Hart	Hard
Hasenfuss	Harefoot (ed)
Hell	Light-colored
Hinterbeine	Hindlegs
Hocke	Hock
Hoden	Testicles
Höhe	Height
Hund	Dog
Hündin	Bitch
Jugend	Youth
Jugendklasse (JKL)	Youth class
Junghund	Puppy
Katzenfuss	Catfeet
Kippohr	Soft ear
Klein	Small
Knocken	Bones
Körbuch	Studbook
Körzucht	Good reproductive qualities
Kruppe	Croup
Kurz	Short
Lang	Long
Länge	Length
Langhaarig	Long coated
Maske (M)	Mask
Muskeln	Muscles
Mutter	Dam
Nachschub	Drive, Thrust
Nagel	Claw
Nase	Nose
Oberarm	Upper arm
Oberschlächtig	Overshot
Ohren	Ears
Pfote	Paw
Rasse	Breed
Rein	Pure
Rot (r)	Red
Rippen	Ribs
Rude (R)	Dog (as against the female)
Sattel (S)	Saddle
Schädel	Skull
Scheu	Shy
Schulter	Shoulder
Schulterblatt	Shoulderblade
Schuss-scheu	Gun-shy
Schussfest	Gun-proof
Schwämmig	Spongy, flabby
Schwanz	Tail
Schwarz (s)	Black
Schwarzgelb (sg)	Black/gold, Black/tan
Schwarzgrau (sgr)	Black/grey
Silbergrau	Silver/grey

German	English	German	English
Steil	Steep	Vorzüglich (V)	Excellent
Stockhaar	Normal coat	Weich	Soft
Tief	Deep	Werfen	Whelp
Traben	Trot, Trotting	Wesen	Temperament
Trocken	Dry	Wesenfest	Firm temperament
Überwinkelt	Over-angulated	Wesenscheu	Shyness
Ungenügend (U)	Unsatisfactory	Wetterfest	Weatherproof
Unterschlächtig	Undershot	Widerrist	Withers
Vater	Sire	Zotthaarig	Open coated
Verein	Club	Zuchtbuch	Studbook
Verkaüflich (Verk)	For Sale	Zuchtbuchnummer	Studbook number
Vorderbeine	Forelegs	Züchter	Breeder
Vorderbrust	Forechest	Zuchtprüfung	Approved (approval)
Vorschub	Reach (of gait)		as suitable for breeding

These are the degree abbreviations most likely to be seen on a German pedigree or catalog, or on a pedigree listing German dogs in the background. The ones marked " x" are obsolete terms and are no longer awarded.

AD		Passed endurance test
BPDH I II	Bahnpolizeidiensthund	Railway Police Dog
BDH x	Bahndiensthund x	Railway Service Dog
BFH	Blindenführhund	Guide Dog for Blind
DH	Diensthund	Working Dog in a Service
DPH	Dienstpolizeihund	Service Police Dog
FH	Fährtenhund	Field Trials Tracking Dog
HGH	Herdengebrauchshund	Herding Dog
Int. Pr. Kl.	Internationale Prüfungsklasse	International Trials Class
Kr.H x	Kriegshund x	War Dog
K.SchH x	Kriegschutzhund x	War Defense Dog or War Guard Dog
LS x	Leistungssieger x	Field Trial Champion
MH I II	Meldehund	Messenger Dog
PFP I II	Polizei-Fahrtenhundprüfung	Police tracking-dog Test
PH	Polizeihund	Police Dog
PDH x	Polizeidiensthund x	Police Dog on Patrol Service
PSP I II	Polizeischutzhund-Prüfung	Police Guard Dog Test
SH I II	Sanitätshund	Red Cross Dog
SchH I II III	Schützhund	Guard or Defense Dog
SuchH x	Suchhund x	Tracking Dog
ZH I II	Zollhund	Customs Dog
ZFH	Zollfährtenhund	Customs Tracker Dog
ZPr.	Zuchtprüfung bestanden	Passed temperament test for breeding.

Note: An " x" *before* a dog's name means that he has been surveyed and passed for breeding.